EDUCATING ACTIVIST ALLIES

Educating Activist Allies offers a fresh take on critical education studies through an analysis of social justice pedagogy in schools serving communities privileged by race and class. By documenting the practices of socially committed teachers at an urban private academy and a suburban public school, Katy Swalwell helps educators and educational theorists better understand the challenges and opportunities inherent in this work. She also examines how students responded to their teachers' efforts in ways that both undermined and realized the goals of social justice pedagogy. This analysis serves as the foundation for the development of a curricular framework helping students to foster an "Activist Ally" identity: the skills, knowledge, and dispositions necessary to negotiate privilege in ways that promote justice. *Educating Activist Allies* provides a powerful introduction to the ways in which social justice curricula can and should be enacted in communities of privilege.

Katy M. Swalwell is Assistant Professor in the College of Education and Human Development at George Mason University, USA.

The Critical Social Thought Series

Edited by Michael W. Apple
University of Wisconsin–Madison

Power and Method
Political Activism and Educational Research
Andrew Gitlin, editor

Critical Ethnography in Educational Research
A Theoretical and Practical Guide
Phil Francis Carspecken

The Uses of Culture
Education and the Limits of Ethnic Affiliation
Cameron McCarthy

Education, Power, and Personal Biography
Dialogues with Critical Educators
Carlos Alberto Torres, editor

Contradictions of School Reform
Educational Costs of Standardized Testing
Linda M. McNeil

Act Your Age!
A Cultural Construction of Adolescence
Nancy Lesko

Tough Fronts
The Impact of Street Culture on Schooling
L. Janelle Dance

Political Spectacle and the Fate of American Schools
Mary Lee Smith with Walter Heinecke, Linda Miller-Kahn, and Patricia F. Jarvis

Rethinking Scientific Literacy
Wolff-Michael Roth and Angela Calabrese Barton

High Stakes Education
Inequality, Globalization, and Urban School Reform
Pauline Lipman

Learning to Labor in New Times
Nadine Dolby and Greg Dimitriadis, editors

Working Method
Research and Social Justice
Lois Weis and Michelle Fine

Class Reunion
The Remaking of the American White Working Class
Lois Weis

Race, Identity, and Representation in Education, Second Edition
Cameron McCarthy, Warren Crichlow, Greg Dimitriadis, and Nadine Dolby

Radical Possibilities
Public Policy, Urban Education, and a New Social Movement
Jean Anyon

Could It Be Otherwise?
Parents and the Inequities of Public School Choice
Lois André-Bechely

Reading and Writing the World with Mathematics
Eric Gustein

Market Movements
African American Involvement in School Voucher Reform
Thomas C. Pedroni

Rightist Multiculturalism
Core Lessons on Neoconservative School Reform
Kristen L. Buras

Unequal by Design
High-Stakes Testing and the Standardization of Inequality
Wayne Au

Black Literate Lives
Historical and Contemporary Perspectives
Maisha T. Fisher

Hidden Markets
The New Education Privatization
Patricia Burch

Critical Perspectives on bell hooks
Maria del Guadalupe Davidson and George Yancy, editors

Advocacy Leadership
Toward a Post-Reform Agenda in Education
Gary L. Anderson

Race, Whiteness, and Education
Zeus Leonardo

Controversy in the Classroom
The Democratic Power of Discussion
Diana E. Hess

The New Political Economy of Urban Education
Neoliberalism, Race, and the Right to the City
Pauline Lipman

Critical Curriculum Studies
Education, Consciousness, and the Politics of Knowing
Wayne Au

Learning to Liberate
Community-Based Solutions to the Crisis in Urban Education
Vajra Watson

Educating Activist Allies
Social Justice Pedagogy with the Suburban and Urban Elite
Katy Swalwell

EDUCATING ACTIVIST ALLIES

Social Justice Pedagogy with the Suburban and Urban Elite

Katy M. Swalwell

 Routledge
Taylor & Francis Group

NEW YORK AND LONDON

KH

First published 2013
by Routledge
711 Third Avenue, New York, NY 10017

Simultaneously published in the UK
by Routledge
2 Park Square, Milton Park, Abingdon, Oxon OX14 4RN

Routledge is an imprint of the Taylor & Francis Group, an informa business

Library of Congress Cataloging-in-Publication Data
Swalwell, Katy M.
Educating activist allies : social justice pedagogy with the suburban and
urban elite / by Katy M. Swalwell.
pages cm. — (The critical social thought series ; 38)
Includes bibliographical references and index.
1. Elite (Social sciences)—Education—United States.
2. Upper class—Education—United States.
3. Critical pedagogy—United States. I. Title.
LC4941.S93 2013
371.82621–dc23   2012037596

ISBN: 978-0-415-52945-7 (hbk)
ISBN: 978-0-415-52946-4 (pbk)
ISBN: 978-0-203-11780-4 (ebk)

Typeset in Bembo
by Cenveo Publisher Services

10/20/14

For my mom, who is always in my heart.

CONTENTS

SERIES EDITOR'S INTRODUCTION

The society in which we live is clearly troubled. Unemployment remains high. Three out of every five jobs that are being created are paid significantly less than before, with fewer benefits, little unionization, and a loss of control over nearly all aspects of one's labor. As if it wasn't bad enough, the latest Census data show that real median income continued its decline. Even more distressing is the fact that now 22% of children in the United States are living in poverty. At the same time, overall poverty increased to over 46 million and nearly 49 million people had no health insurance, a figure that would be even higher were it not for the health reforms instituted by the Obama government. Yet the income gap between the wealthiest 20% of US households and the rest of us grew sharply. To make it even more stark, the top 5% of the population saw an additional 5% gain in wealth. This was on top of the massive gains they had already received during the last decade (see Harris, 2012; Tavernise, 2012). All of these figures are even more distressing when race is taken into account, clearly documenting the racializing nature of the institutional structures that organize this society (Leonardo 2009; Tavernise, 2012).

There are a number of important things to realize from these data. The first is the deep seated nature of inequality, and that inequality is worsening over the years. The second, less visible, point is that these are official government data, data that historically have tended to under-report the actual conditions of impoverishment and despair that exist in so many parts of the nation. Thus, the figures on real unemployment may need to be nearly doubled, with youth, people of color, and many impoverished women suffering even more.

In the face of these conditions, what can education do? Dominant groups have a particular set of visions of what is wrong with this society and a particular set of formulaic responses to what education must do in these times. We are being told that education is both the source of and the cure for an entire range of things that are wrong in this society. Schools and the teachers within them are under concerted attack. The answers being offered include such things as marketization and competition, standardization of curricula and ever more testing, performance pay for teachers, and so many more proposals that it's hard to keep up. There is actually little robust evidence that any of these proposals actually work in the long run (Apple, 2006). Further, these policies are constantly being contested in large and small ways in communities and schools throughout the nation (see Lipman, 2011). Indeed, even in the face of criticisms from well-known educators who had previously supported these dominant policies and who are now totally opposed to them (Ravitch, 2011), the avalanche of "reforms" still keeps coming.

But are these the only educational responses that are possible or available. Here the answer is a resounding "No." There is a rich set of approaches that have been developed and used in schools and communities throughout this nation and many others. These embody very different kinds of norms, ones involving critically democratic education. Both of these words—critical and democratic—are important. The educational policies and practices that are embodied in these approaches illuminate and contest dominant power relations inside and outside of education. But they do so in ways that restore the agency of teachers and students. They are indeed deeply critical. However, pedagogically their aim is not to simply replace one unquestioned dominant ideology with another.

These more critical approaches have a very long theoretical and practical history (see, e.g., Apple, Au, and Gandin, 2009). Some are based in the influential work of the great Brazilian educator Paulo Freire. Others come from critical educational practices developed by community activists, cultural workers, and teachers in schools throughout the United States. But no matter where they come from, each of them is deeply committed to an education for social justice and to a set of egalitarian values that sees people—including students, teachers, and communities—as co-responsible subjects. Katy Swalwell and the fine book you are about to read are situated in a long history of educators asking and answering the question of whether and in what ways schools can play a role in social transformation (Apple, 2013).

One of the criticisms of the literature on "critical pedagogy" is that it is often so theoretical, and written in such convoluted ways, that its very style makes it very hard for educators to see where they might enter into it. This will not do. We need powerful analyses of how to do critical work and how to do it with different kinds of students and in different kinds of settings.

There are places to which many critically democratic educators have turned for rich descriptions of what is possible in a time of conservative attacks on schools and teachers. The journal *Rethinking Schools* continues to be a center for the promotion of critical educational work. Popular books such as *Democratic Schools* (Apple and Beane, 2007) also have given teachers and administrators, many of whom are deeply dissatisfied with what they are told to do, detailed looks at classrooms and entire schools that are using critically democratic policies and practices to make a major difference in the lives of their students and in the communities in which they are embedded (see also Gutstein, 2006). Even more recently, Vajra Watson has shown what this looks like in community-based education (Watson, 2012).

Much of the emphasis in critical education has been on poor and oppressed populations and this is true of most of the material to which I pointed in my previous paragraph. In no way do I wish to diminish the crucial importance of the hard work that teachers, community workers, and so many others continue to do to build an engaging, culturally responsive, and socially critical education with these students. However, because so much attention is rightly given to the poor and disenfranchised and to those whom this society has marginalized as the "Other," less attention has been paid to critical education for those who benefit the most from this society's dominant institutions and power relations, what Katy Swalwell calls the "suburban and urban elite."

This is a distinct problem. All sets of social relations are just that—relations. For there to be the "poor" there is a corresponding category of the "affluent." For there to be "people of color" there is a corresponding category of people who see themselves as the "human ordinary"—"White." This simple point has considerable political bite. There is not a poor problem unless there is a rich problem. There is less of a Black problem than there is a White problem. Less of a gay problem than a straight problem. Less of a women's problem than a men's problem.

This has important implications for education and for Swalwell's book. It asks us not only to focus on those who are oppressed by this society's dominant power relations, but to also pay considerably more attention to those who are situated in classed, gender, and raced positions that give them more advantages because of that very location.

Among the tasks of the critical scholar/activist in education are: 1) to tell the truth about the nature of the inequalities in this society; 2) to show where there are opportunities, spaces, for engaging in work that challenges these inequalities; and 3) to act as critical secretaries of those individuals and groups who are engaged in the creative and hard practical efforts of actually successfully acting on these challenges (Apple, 2013). *Educating Activist Allies* does all three and does them well. It is grounded in a substantive understanding of the ways this society is organized to produce massive inequalities in power and resources and in how schools fit into these relations. It illuminates the spaces in schools where teachers have maintained their autonomy and where they can engage in critical pedagogic and curricular work. And, finally, it provides us with detailed portraits of what committed critical educational work looks like in classrooms.

But this is not all. Swalwell is a fine writer, someone who does all of this with theoretical elegance and insightful accounts that draw the reader in to the lives of real teachers and students in real communities. She takes us inside the classrooms of two dedicated and talented teachers, both of whom are working in affluent areas with more economically advantaged students. We go with them on their class trips. We sit in on their intense discussions of the unequal relations that characterize this society and of the issues of their own personal responsibility in such a society. We see how teachers constantly try to create an educational environment where serious critical ethical and political insights are natural parts of the curriculum and teaching in their classrooms.

Swalwell is not content to simply be an observer. Her final chapter draws important lessons from these teachers' classrooms for those educators who wish to engage in the creative and fulfilling work of doing critically democratic education. In the process, *Educating Activist Allies* provides us with steps that will enable us to go forward. In so doing, it also helps us to then tell those who wish to turn education into training—and who have forgotten what an education worthy of its name might be—that there *are* realistic alternatives to the lamentable policies now being all too readily imposed on the schools and teachers of this nation and all too many others.

Michael W. Apple
John Bascom Professor of Curriculum and
Instruction and Educational Policy Studies
University of Wisconsin–Madison

References

Apple, M. (2006). *Educating the 'Right' way: Markets, standards, God, and inequality*. New York: Routledge.

Apple, M.W. (2013). *Can education change society?* New York: Routledge.

Apple, M.W., Au, W., and Gandin, L.A. (Eds.) (2009). *The Routledge international handbook of critical education*. New York: Routledge.

Apple, M.W. and Beane, J.A. (Eds.) (2007). *Democratic schools: Lessons in powerful education*, 2nd ed. Portsmouth, NH: Heinemann.

Gutstein, E. (2006). *Reading and writing the world with mathematics: Toward a pedagogy for social justice*. New York: Routledge.

Harris, P. (2012). US Census figures show more than one in five children are living in poverty. *Guardian*. September 13. www.guardian.co.uk/business/2012/se/12/us-census-figures-children-poverty. Downloaded September 13, 2012, 2:15pm.

Leonardo, Z. (2009). *Race, whiteness, and education*. New York: Routledge.

Lipman, P. (2011). *The new political economy of education: Neoliberalism, race, and the right to the city*. New York: Routledge.

Ravitch, D. (2011). *The death and life of the great American school system: How testing and choice are undermining education*. New York: Basic Books.

Tavernise, S. (2012). US income gap rose, sign of uneven recovery. *New York Times*, September 12. www.nytimes.com/2012/09/13/us/us-incomes-dropped-last-year-census-bureau. Downloaded September 13, 2012, 2:00pm.

Watson, V. (2012). *Learning to liberate: Community based solutions to the crisis in urban education*. New York: Routledge.

ACKNOWLEDGMENTS

No one ever writes a book alone or, at least, they shouldn't. A litany of loved ones diligently kept me focused throughout this process when I needed to buckle down and distracted me when I needed a break. Heath Henderson, Rachael Goodman, and Kate and Brian Mitchell (along with their daughter, Abby) have gallantly borne the brunt of these duties this past year with patience and humor. In addition, my sister, Abbey Henderson, and my dad, Rick Swalwell, have logged over thirty years of inspiring and supporting me. Without complaint, they (and their wonderful spouses, Eric and Karen) fielded numerous phone calls at varying stress levels and welcomed me home whenever I needed to get away. I am ridiculously lucky to have you all in my life and love you very much.

I also owe an enormous debt of gratitude to those family, friends, and colleagues who took time to read and think about my work in its many stages. Though not an exhaustive list (and my apologies to anyone I have forgotten), the following people deserve special thanks: Janel Anderson, Michael Apple, Wayne Au, Kristen Buras, Alexa Dimick, Joe Ferrare, Daniel Friedrich, Naomi Fynboh, Lauren Gatti, Paul Gorski, Diana Hess, Mary Klehr, Courtney Koestler, Miriam Kopelow, Kerry Kretchmar, Jane Mlenar, Adam Nelson, Kate O'Connor, Mariana Pacheco, Katie Payne, Judy Perez, Joyce Rupp, Rob Sanders, Simone Schweber, Beth Sondel, Samantha Spinney, Ann Van Etten, Jenice View, Anita Wager, Quentin Wheeler-Bell, and all the past and present members of Friday Group at the University of Wisconsin–Madison. Their suggestions, critiques, questions, and curiosity have been both personally and professionally sustaining. Given that my work is markedly better for having crossed their paths, I also thank them on behalf of my editors and readers. Speaking of editors, I would be remiss if I did not mention Catherine Bernard, Allison Bush and Emily How who have been enormously gracious (and patient) in helping to prepare this book for publication.

Lastly, I want to thank the students who participated in this study as well as Vernon Sloan and Liz Johnson, two exceptional educators who continue to inspire me in my personal and professional life and whose real identities I wish I could reveal in order to properly acknowledge them. It is no doubt unnerving to welcome a stranger into your classroom who may critique and analyze your every move, yet they rarely hesitated to invite me "behind-the-scenes" and let me in on their hopes, fears, and challenges. This book would quite simply not have been possible without their generosity and openness and I genuinely enjoyed our time together. From the bottom of my heart, thank you.

INTRODUCTION

A few years ago, I presented a workshop entitled "Addressing Wealth Inequality with Students in Affluent Communities" at the Northwest Teachers for Social Justice Conference. A wonderful event that can inspire even the most demoralized of educators, it is well worth the trip to Portland, Oregon. As I turned on the overhead projector and collated handouts before the session began, I wondered if my focus on affluent students would attract anyone among a group of such committed and talented social justice educators. I was stunned (and relieved) when the room filled to capacity with curious conference attendees.

One by one, the teachers introduced themselves and shared why they had come to the session. Almost all of them worked at private or suburban public schools primarily serving White students from affluent families. They expressed frustration with how to challenge their students' meritocratic perceptions of the world. They gave examples of student apathy, willful ignorance, or missionary zeal in response to a social justice curriculum. And they talked of pushback to their teaching from parents, administrators, and fellow colleagues. Perhaps most movingly, they expressed gratitude for a space to talk about doing this work with these kids. "I'm embarrassed to say where I teach when I come to things like this," one teacher told me. "It's like if I really cared about social justice, then I shouldn't be working in this kind of school."

The education of children from communities of privilege is admittedly not a particularly common or popular approach for those committed to social justice education.[1] There is no doubt that students from low-income families and students of color are among those most deeply and immediately hurt by the increasing stratification and segregation of society made worse by a "conservative modernization" that drives American schooling at the macro and micro levels (Apple, 2006). Schools are not simply sites of opportunity; rather they are deeply political places where students are sorted and labeled and where the policies, practices, curricula, and informal interactions can reproduce society's inequalities in both covert and unambiguous ways (Oakes, 2005).

To those who are both aware and critical of this state of affairs, it may seem antithetical to work in schools celebrated for their success as defined by test scores and matriculation rates. These are places where nothing is perceived as broken, the curriculum is rarely questioned, and injustice is perceived as something that happens somewhere else. At these schools, students' obliviousness to oppression and their relationship to it is maintained by "teachers, preachers, parents, and the mass media to which they are daily subjected [who] have made the choice to lie to them, either directly or by omission" (Wise, 2008, p. xi). Rather than give up and cede that pedagogic space to others in the face of such powerful reproductive forces, however, there are educators who choose to work in communities of privilege and who attempt to use whatever influence they possess to interrupt social injustices at the individual and structural level. Teachers committed to social justice at such schools may be challenged by their colleagues who are unaware or accepting of the status quo as well as by their justice-oriented peers from other schools who question their decision to work in non-marginalized communities.

This book is for those teachers and for those who help them develop. It is to help them open students' eyes to the world around them, even when they are reluctant to see things that are painful, disturbing, or in contradiction with their original beliefs about the world. There is much teachers can do to help students as they encounter new, strange, and troubling information. By describing and analyzing the experiences of social justice teachers and their students from two social studies classrooms at an elite private academy and a suburban public school, I hope I can remind these educators that they are not alone, share ideas for improving their own practices, and make a case for why they are an important part of the social justice education community.

As I wrote this book, I tried to see the text from the perspectives of classroom teachers and teacher educators by including that which they might find most helpful and organizing it in ways they might find most useful.[2] Thus, I have divided the book into two parts with chapters that can be read in order or in isolation. In Part I, I attempt to answer two questions: why is it important to consider the education of children in privileged communities, and how should they be educated? In Chapter 1, "Why the Education of Privileged Children Matters," I explain what I mean by "privilege" and outline several reasons why social justice educators, indeed all of us, ought to care about the ways in which and to what ends we educate privileged children: to better understand how inequalities persist, to be strategic about harnessing the power they inherit, and to demonstrate concern for them as sufferers of dehumanization. In Chapter 2, "Disconnected, Paralyzed, and Charitable: Social Justice Pedagogy with Privileged Children," I explain what I mean by social justice pedagogy and review the potential for such curriculum and instruction to backfire with students. Rather than cultivate a deep awareness of injustice, a sense of empowerment, and alliances with marginalized groups, the current research base points to privileged youth's feelings of disconnection, paralysis from guilt or anger when implicated in injustice, and participation in unidirectional charity.

Part II attempts to understand how these undesirable outcomes might be rectified by examining the experiences of social justice teachers and their students in suburban and urban elite educational settings. Chapter 3, "Sheltered and Exceptional: Privileged Students' Conceptions of Themselves and Their Communities," investigates the impact of social class and place on students' perceptions of their communities. For example, middle-class suburban students thought of themselves as living within a bubble while upper-class urban students thought of themselves as exceptional members of a privileged class at ease within the world. Chapter 4, "Social Justice Pedagogy in Action: 'Bursting the Bubble' and 'Disturbing the Comfortable'" explores the divergent philosophies of two social justice teachers whose classrooms serve as critical ethnographic case studies that highlight strategies to address the inherent tensions within social justice pedagogy with privileged children. Of particular interest is how teachers negotiated fusing college prep with social justice teaching, exposing students to multiple perspectives as well as social critique, and balancing pragmatism with idealism when making pedagogic decisions.

Chapter 5, "Did They Get It?: Privileged Students' Responses to Social Justice Pedagogy," examines students' interpretations of their social responsibilities with regards to injustice in ways that both reproduced and re-networked their privilege. I introduce four "modes of thinking" that represent students' ideas about justice and privilege: the Meritocrat, the Benevolent Benefactor, the Resigned, and the Activist Ally. This chapter also draws attention to the unique experiences of working-class students, students of color, and politically conservative students in these classrooms. The book concludes with Chapter 6, "Eyes Pried Open: A Framework for Educating Activist Allies," in which I introduce a model of social justice pedagogy with children from privileged communities based upon an analysis of the common characteristics among activities that tended to elicit an Activist Ally mode of thinking among students. I conclude the chapter with several practical steps to assist teachers and teacher educators hoping to effectively implement this model.

Though the focus of this book is students with access to economic and racial privilege, I recognize the need to trouble the binary of "privileged" and "marginalized" when enacting or analyzing social justice education. Rather than approach students' identities as fixed positions, this work is rooted in the idea that people's "intersecting" identities are contradictory and context-specific (Edwards, 2006; Curry-Stevens, 2007). Though their experiences are unique enough to warrant focused attention, it is important to remember that the lessons here are not only intended for segregated classes of White, affluent students who may be classified as "net beneficiaries" of privilege, but rather ought to be a means for students from all backgrounds to examine how systems position people in ways that benefit and marginalize them, to identify the contexts in which they are positioned as beneficiaries, and to practice how to use such power in ways that advance justice. To all those educators engaged in such work, I wish you luck and hope this volume is a helpful guide.

Notes

1 I outline more specifically what I mean by "privilege" and what I mean by "social justice education" in the next chapter.
2 I was a classroom teacher for several years and am now a teacher educator working primarily within communities of privilege. For an overview of my background and how it influenced the collection and analysis of data for this book, see Appendix A.

PART I

The Education of Privileged Youth in Theory

1

WHY THE EDUCATION OF PRIVILEGED CHILDREN MATTERS

> In the egoistic pursuit of having as a possessing class, [the oppressors] suffocate in
> their own possessions and no longer are; they merely have.
>
> *(Freire, 2000, p. 58)*

It is possible that if I surveyed a group of educational scholars and practitioners, a majority would respond with a quick and firm "we shouldn't" to the question of whether we ought to be concerned with the education of elite children. For the record, I am not unsympathetic to this position as there are many other populations of students whose schooling is clearly in crisis. And yet, I find this question to be not so easy to dismiss. For me, it hangs in the air, lurking in the shadows of conversations about justice and equity in education, buried deep in the assumptions of current educational reforms, and haunting the critical reflections of my own schooling. If we begin to entertain this question, if we let it linger, we soon find that it begets other even more difficult and important questions: How should these students be educated? What happens when we try to educate them in those ways?

Why Ask This Question Now?

Before providing a few possible answers to this fundamental question of why we ought to care about the education of elite children, and before diving into stories about how these students can and should be educated, we must first position this inquiry in a particular context of time and space. I write this from the United States at the end of the first decade of the 21st century when a widening gap between the rich and poor and increasing *de facto* segregation are startlingly harsh realities playing out amidst mythic claims of living in a "post-racial" society where anyone can get ahead if they work hard. While political debates rage about why economic and racial inequalities persist and what ought to be done about them, few debate this basic truth: in fundamental ways, the United States is becoming more separate and less equal.

Despite recent Supreme Court decisions effectively disavowing a need for race-conscious educational policies (e.g., *Parents v. Seattle School District*, *Meredith v. Jefferson County*), public schools nationwide struggle with significant and increasing economic and racial segregation (Orfield, Frankenberg, & Garces, 2008). As more White families enroll their children in suburban, charter, and private schools with little exposure to students (or teachers) from other racial groups (Frankenberg, Siegel-Hawley, & Wang, 2010), more students of color are siphoned into under-funded "hyper-segregated" or "apartheid schools" in the country's large urban centers (Frankenberg, Lee, & Orfield, 2003). Though the stereotypical White, wealthy suburb on the outskirts of a diverse, working-class urban center is changing,[1] racial homogeneity for White students is still the norm. In fact, the average White student attends a school where 77% of the student body is also White (Orfield, 2009). Underlying economic inequalities exacerbate this racial segregation. For example, as of 2009, 43% of Black and Hispanic students attended schools with poverty rates over 80% while fewer than 4% of White children attended such schools (McArdle, Osypuk, & Acevedo-García, 2010). Overall, Black families earn a median income that is 58% of Whites' (Isaacs, 2007), are much less likely to experience economic mobility than Whites (Sharkey, 2009), and have disproportionately felt the negative effects of the recent foreclosure epidemic (Rothstein, 2012).

Mobility has decreased for all racial/ethnic groups, however, as the correlation between productivity and income has unhinged for the working class (Sawhill & Morton, 2007; Allegretto, 2011). Simply put, the current gap between the rich and the poor is one of the widest ever in American history. While the average American household saw their earnings increase about 25% in the past forty years, the income of the richest 5% has increased by 68%, the top 1% by 323% and the richest one-tenth of a percent by 492% (Khan, 2011). A recent Economic Policy Institute report notes that the top 5% of households currently control 63.5% of the nation's wealth (Allegretto, 2011). To make matters worse, it is not just that the rich are getting richer: the poor are getting poorer (Bernstein, McNichols, & Nicholas, 2008). Though some may defend a system capable of producing such wildly disparate wealth as a meritocracy that rewards "hard work," this kind of gap is socially corrosive and fundamentally unstable (Pickett & Wilkinson, 2009). It is also unlikely to change soon given steeply rising education, health care, and energy costs coupled with a push to privatize or eliminate many social safety nets.

These worrisome statistics demonstrate that, at the very least, whether or not we should care about the education of privileged children is not an irrelevant topic: such students exist and their privilege (particularly with regards to their economic security) is intensifying. Before justifying why we indeed ought to care about how they are educated, however, we must first address the problematic nature of a category like "privilege" given the multiplicity of ways that all of us experience advantage or marginalization to some degree.

Who Is Privileged?

A discourse of privilege within social justice circles has emerged in the last several decades from a rejection of traditional justice-based work focusing on the oppression of particular groups towards a deconstruction of the ways in which dominant groups maintain and reproduce power (i.e., studying the ways in which men actively reproduce sexism as well as researching women's experiences of oppression) (Bonnett, 1996; Choules, 2007). With her landmark article "Unpacking the White Knapsack," Peggy McIntosh (1990) is probably the most famous example of how someone adopting a position of privilege (in her case, White privilege) finds herself made newly accountable to those whose oppression benefits her. Postcolonial, postmodern, cultural, and critical theorists have also been quite productive in problematizing traditional liberal and conservative understandings of oppression and privilege, particularly with regards to male privilege and Whiteness (e.g., McIntosh, 1997).

A variety of terms with different connotations has surfaced: terms that de-center privileged people like *non-marginalized*, terms that indicate active intent like *oppressor* and *dominator*, and terms that imply an invisible hand producing inequality like *advantaged*, *privileged*, and *dominant*. An emerging field offers work focusing on a *pedagogy for the non-poor* (Evans, A., Evans, R., & Kennedy, 1995), *pedagogy of the oppressor* (Schapiro, 1999), *pedagogy for the children of the oppressors* (van Gorder, 2007), or *education for the privileged* (Goodman, 2000a, 2000b). Because of their prevalence, I have adopted the terms *communities of privilege* and *privileged*, with the hope that they encourage "the beneficiaries of injustice to see themselves as implicated and having some collective responsibility for the perpetuation of injustice" (Choules, 2007, p. 474).

I adopt this discourse with great caution, however, in an attempt to listen to the insightful critiques from scholars who warn that the term "privilege(d)" obscures the subject of domination by describing oppression as happening without the knowledge of the oppressors. For example, Hernández-Sheets (2000) critiques the use of this "nice word" in relation to race as a "benevolent and socially imposed prerogative of Whites … [that] can reinforce feelings of superiority and help construct personal and group identities based on the devaluation of others" (p. 19). To avoid the use of a term that reinforces injustice, critical race scholars recommend a discourse of "supremacy" that acknowledges privilege, but only, in the case of race, as a "function of whites' actions toward minority subjects and not as mysterious accumulations of unearned advantages" (Leonardo, 2009, pp. 89–90). If it weren't so cumbersome, I would rather identify elite or privileged students as those positioned by power relations within systems of supremacy that are continuously shaped by historical social, political, and economic factors and that are made stronger when rendered invisible, consciously or not, to those who benefit from them most. To prevent reader fatigue, however, I use the term *privileged* as shorthand for this long-winded clarification.

Traditionally, scholars have made sense of privilege as a set of unearned advantages based upon socially constructed categories (e.g., race, gender, sexual orientation) within which people are largely unable to avoid benefiting from regardless of their level of consciousness. While it may be tempting to tally privileges in an additive fashion, "our social identities are not a balance sheet in which one can just compare the number of identities on the dominant side and the number on the subordinate side and know how much power, privilege, or freedom one has" (Goodman, 2000b, pp. 32–22). Such a commodified understanding of privilege is rightly being complicated by a new generation of scholars focusing less on the unequal benefits enjoyed by "privileged" people and more on the unjust processes of privileging as socio-culturally mediated identity formation and its related distribution of resources (e.g., Howard, 2008; Khan, 2011).

Rather than a set of clear-cut, fixed characteristics, then, privilege represents a context-dependent, mediated process by which fluid dynamics produce complex, sometimes contradictory, identities (Brantlinger, 2003; Johnson, 2006; Curry-Stevens, 2007; Denis-McKay, 2007; Leonardo, 2009). Such a situated process of privilege serves as a lens that shapes and maintains values, perceptions, thoughts, feelings, and actions regarding one's self in relation to others. Rather than someone simply identifying as "marginalized" or "privileged" writ large, what is more likely is an "intersecting identity" (Edwards, 2006) or "modified binary framework" wherein aspects of one's multiple identities interact in concert with others' identities and the situation at hand to either "moderate or exacerbate an experience of privilege, on one hand, and oppression, on the other" (Curry-Stevens, 2007, p. 37). In my case, for example, the ability to claim membership in dominant racial, social class, sexual identity, citizenship status, and physical ability groups positions me in powerful ways in most situations; conversely, my gender, home region, and religious background at times (and in relation to certain people) tend to position me more outside the margins of power.

Several scholars outline aspects of this privileging/marginalization process to help identify who is privileged and who is marginalized in a given situation. Goodman (2000b) helpfully distinguishes among the characteristics of privileged *individuals* and privileged *groups*. Privileged individuals are those who lack consciousness regarding privilege and its benefits, who easily deny or avoid the privileging process, and who maintain a sense of superiority and entitlement that their needs should be met even when it is at the expense of oppressed people. Similarly, Hackman's (2005) taxonomy identifies *dominants* as people who are actively taught not to see their privilege, who believe that their life and its privileges are the norm for society and humanity, and who have done nothing to earn the benefits that accompany privilege.

Privileged groups, on the other hand, are those which maintain cultural and institutional domination by creating structures and systems that reflect and promote the internalization of privileged values, normalize their values and beliefs by supporting particular policies and practices, believe in the superiority of their values, and actively grant material and psychological benefits to their peers at the expense of subjugated groups. This process does not require nefarious intentions to work; in ways both subtle and explicit, these systems condition people to think of themselves as normal (Goodman, 2000b; Johnson, 2006) and to make small allowances for critiques in order to silence them (Buras, 2008).

Ultimately, all of us embody traits by which these forces oppress and privilege us based upon aspects of our personhood deemed important for membership in subordinate or dominant groups. Though these identities are complex, fluid (to a point), and relationally situated, it is important to recognize that there do exist people who, in general, garner unearned advantage in most situations and who more often than not can claim association with elite groups. These people, and I would include myself in this category, are *net beneficiaries* of privilege who, "because of their positioning within the dominant group at both a local and/or global level, attract privilege of different sorts [granting the] ability to act without consequences and as if one had the right to set the rules" (Choules, 2007, p. 461, 472). In other words, these are people who have the "luxury of obliviousness" (Johnson, 2006). Conversely, there are people who dominant groups consistently marginalize and whose actions are severely constrained regardless of context—*net maleficiaries*.[2]

It is important to note that acknowledging the ways in which one is not permanently privileged does not justify a relativist stance whereby all people oppress and are oppressed so that everyone is equal in a sort of injustice wash. On the contrary, there are individuals who claim membership in certain groups that tend to be unjustly favored by hegemonic forces at the macro and micro levels in ways that make a deep and lasting difference. To claim otherwise is arrogant at worst and ignorant at best, especially if one's "knapsack," as Peggy McIntosh (1990) would say, is very full. For the purposes of this project, then, these net beneficiaries are referred to as privileged people while net maleficiaries (those whose experiences in the aggregate tend to deny them access to resources and opportunities) are referred to as marginalized people. These experiences of domination and oppression take a variety of powerful forms including sexual orientation, physical ability, and gender.[3] In American society, however, there are few ways in which this process of privileging operates more powerfully than by the racialization of people and their stratification by social class.

Race

Recent advances in genetic technologies prove beyond the shadow of a doubt that race is not a biological truth (Templeton, 1999), but rather a social construction that originiated out of a desire to distribute power based upon hierarchies that favored White over Black identities. For as deeply embedded as it is in society, "Whiteness" is a relatively new yet nefarious category that has grown more powerful through conscious legislation and deliberate actions beginning with the colonization of the Americas when laws granting rights distinguished between enslaved African people and indentured servants of European heritage (Lipsitz, 2002; Johnson, 2006). There is a rich and complex history of immigrants struggling with how to negotiate the connection between Whiteness and citizenship, particularly among those from Ireland, Greece, Italy, India, and a range of Latin American countries. Often, people from these regions have been compelled to distance themselves rather than ally with Black peoples in order to gain social and economic advantages (e.g., Foley, 2002). Historically, legislation has encouraged such divisiveness in order to support systems of White supremacy (Lipsitz, 2002). Throughout the history of the United States, becoming "American" has thus often been conflated with becoming "White" (Barrett & Roediger, 2002).

In the past thirty years, growing attention to Whiteness as a socio-historical phenomenon has resulted in a sub-discipline of "White studies." There seem to be at least three approaches to this field: a deconstructive analysis of Whiteness from a social and historical perspective (e.g., Dyer, 1988), a call for the total abolition of Whiteness (e.g., Garvey & Ignatiev, 1997), and the advocacy of a re-articulation of Whiteness (e.g., Kincheloe & Steinberg, 1998, Leonardo, 2009). In thinking about social justice pedagogy with people typically privileged by their racial identity, I advocate re-articulation based on a deconstructive analysis that "examines whiteness in relation to oppression and domination and as a viable, progressive, and contradictory category" (Rodriguez, 2000, p. 16). This position rejects calls for abolition given that such an approach tends to ignore how deeply embedded race is in society, overlooks the differences within Whiteness (e.g., the marginalization of people referred to as "White trash"), and, ironically, may strengthen the flawed position that race does not matter which can unwittingly lead to the srengthening of White supremacy (Rodriguez, 2000).

Social Class

In addition to and often in conjunction with this history of racialization in the United States are the deep influences of an economic system grounded in the principles of a competitive market system. Modern capitalism is rooted in the sixteenth-century rise of Western European profit-sharing corporations engaged in high-risk investments to compete for control over natural and human resources in Africa and the Americas. The growth of such an economic system depended upon the exploitation of cheap and free labor in the forms of indentured and enslaved peoples as well as cheap resources, including the conquest of indigenous peoples and their territories through military means and imperialist political agendas (Marx, 1990; Wright, 1997).

We live today with the result of these efforts: the United States is among the wealthiest of nations in the world yet struggles with a history of indigenous genocide, slavery, segregation, and increasingly high numbers of people living below the poverty line. It has also produced a fairly fixed class structure: a small yet extremely rich capitalist and corporate managerial class, an unstable middle class whose position is tied to training in technical skills for jobs with particular credentials, a large working class rapidly losing any former protections they may have had through unionization, a segment of this working class with little to no job security, and a thoroughly marginalized poor whose living conditions make it virtually impossible to acquire the skills and education needed for jobs to lift them out of poverty (Wright and Rogers, 2010).[4] Throughout American history, varying degrees of regulation, taxation, and other policies have attempted to address these issues, but rarely has capitalism itself been questioned (Mattick, 2011).

When thinking about who is a net beneficiary of racial privilege, those who can claim Whiteness are clear candidates for such a status. Thinking about people who are privileged by capitalism, on the other hand, is a bit more complicated yet clearly important in that class distinctions create "unequal possibilities for flourishing and suffering" (Sayer, 2005, p. 218). Scholars thinking about social class are not in agreement about how to describe an "inherently indescribable concept" (Conley, 2008, p. 367). It is not simply a matter of how much income a family generates (Lareau, 2008) nor whether someone is an employee or the employer (Wright, 1997), though clearly how much money people have, how people earn their money, and what people do with their money are all important aspects of social class (Hout, 2008).

For the purposes of this book, I focus on those children from families who identify themselves at the top tiers of Wright and Rogers' (2010) taxonomy: the capitalist and corporate managerial class and those in more stable upper-middle-class positions. I also take into account Conley's (2008) "folk concept" of class, the ways in which laypeople think about class that include the trajectories related to someone's education, occupation, and income. It should come as no surprise that this approach can produce complex identities for people (e.g., the factory foreman without a college education who owns multiple rental properties or the attorney with little disposable income because of large student loans and alimony payments). My focus, however, is on those individuals in "clear class positions" whose racial and class status most often align and who tend to leverage them as a means for moving into homogenous "good" neighborhoods filled with similarly classed and raced people (Pattillo, 2008).

Whether focusing on race or social class, we are wise to remember that the two are intimately bound (in both historical and contemporary terms) in what Johnson (2006) calls a "matrix of domination" and what Pattillo (2008) refers to as "inflection" in that class "inflects" race. Leonardo (2009), too, poetically connects advanced capitalism with Whiteness (and patriarchy) as "the hour and minute hands of a clock so predictable, it should not surprise the critical educator that where you find one, the other lurks closely behind" (p. 182). Historical examples abound of these categories' connections: the enslavement of African people for free labor, the prevention of unity among working-class peoples by hiring strikebreakers from competing racial/ethnic groups, and current debates about immigration centering around "those people" taking "our jobs." Throughout this book, there are times when I focus more on race or more on class and times when I lump the two together. In all cases, I acknowledge that the ways in which someone may be positioned differently in relation to both categories no doubt influences their experiences of "privilege."

I want to reiterate that we are all complicated beings whose multi-layered identities influence our lives to varying degrees in a variety of contexts. Though it is clear that a privileged identity is neither fixed nor binary, we cannot ignore the existence of privilege along evolving racial and class lines as a powerful process. Neither can we avoid addressing its unjust consequences, particularly with those students who tend to embody the characteristics that make them net beneficiaries (i.e., students who can claim Whiteness and who come from middle-/upper-class families).

What Do We Know about the Education of Privileged Children?

With this conception of privilege in mind, I want to clarify what I mean by an elite education and outline what we know about its effects on privileged children. In keeping with my definition of privilege, I define an elite education as the schooling that children experience and expect as one of the benefits granted them by their membership in a privileged social group. For example, children from privileged backgrounds, especially those related to social class, have parents/ guardians able to move them into neighborhoods with access to safe, stable, high-achieving public schools or simply pay for a reputable private school. In other words, whether public or private, privileged schools have barriers to entry (explicit and implicit) that help them to serve both as markers of and makers of privilege.[5]

By most conventional measures, students who attend private and public schools serving communities of privilege appear to be doing well; in general, they tend to get good grades, graduate, and matriculate to institutions of higher education. To be sure, these children have received ample resources and attention and are indeed likely to succeed in a variety of ways. It may seem absurd to identify them as an at-risk group in any way when contrasted with students from marginalized groups who struggle to demonstrate what they know on standardized tests, are pushed or drop out of schools, do not graduate from college, etc. These are students whose schooling is clearly in crisis and whose needs demand immediate attention in ways that students in privileged communities do not (e.g., Valenzuela, 1999;

Meiners, 2007). In no way am I advocating that the actions of activists and teachers, the gaze of researchers, or the efforts of policymakers ought to ignore these issues.

I do, however, claim that students from communities of privilege face challenges that merit further investigation. Very few scholars have empirically or theoretically looked up the social ladder to understand the education of these youth. The work of Anyon (1980), Bourdieu (1984), Lipman (1998), Brantlinger (2003), and Lareau (2003) are notable exceptions that provide important insights into the way privilege is reproduced through, inscribed upon, and experienced by people from dominant groups.[6] Recently, there has been a burst of ethnographic activity studying elite private day and boarding schools (Howard, 2008; Gaztambide-Fernández, 2009; Khan, 2011) following in the footsteps of Cookson & Persell (1985), as well as an attempt to understand the mechanisms at work in Ivy League college admissions (Karabel, 2006; Stevens, 2007). Building on the work of Kingston and Lewis (1990), Howard and Gaztambide-Fernández's (2010) edited volume, *Educating Elites: Class Privilege and Educational Advantage*, is a particularly useful compendium.

What this recent scholarship tells us about the education of privileged youth is that they are often cultivated to appear capable of independently juggling multiple responsibilities and to engage in intense competition with the aplomb of a professional. Parents and teachers in privileged communities tend to "concertedly cultivate" their children (Lareau, 2003), which results in students rarely feeling safe to make mistakes or take the risk inherent in creative and critical thinking (Howard, 2008). In his recent ethnographic work exploring schooling at St. Paul's Academy, for example, Khan (2011) found that teachers and White students naturalized social hierarchies as artifacts of a meritocratic ladder system. Students pointed to their diverse range of experiences rather than their heritage in order to justify their position near the top, actively ignoring the deep relationship between the two. As a result, successful students expressed an embodied sense of ease and an attitude of radical egalitarianism in terms of their cultural tastes rather than a sense of entitlement marked by cultural distinctions of "high" culture. Not surprisingly, upper-class straight White male students succeeded more frequently in this system than did students who identified as working class, LGBTQ, female, or from a racial background other than White.

Regardless of their demographic descriptors, what we know from the small body of empirical work about these students is that those who excel within privileged school settings tend to be those who embrace hierarchies, ignore structural inequalities, and demonstrate egalitarianism and politeness on the surface with a streak of independence and competitiveness just below. Denis-McKay (2007), for example, describes a poignant example of one little boy in her class at an international school in Mali and challenges his "successful" identity in school when he refuses her assignment to write a thank you note to someone who had helped him:

Although this student was academically talented and demonstrated academic success over and over, he was unable to critically reflect on his own culture, indeed his own position in life, and he was certainly unable to connect or form community. A child of great privilege in a land of need, he had been cared for by nannies, cooks, butlers, and guardians. His parents hired many people to provide care. They were unable to buy caring, however, and this student was stunted in his ability to be critically reflective about the "morally neutral" ground of his privilege, as well as his ability to form connection and community.

(p. 31)

Additionally, this schooling perpetuates other beliefs that are undesirable to advocates of social justice pedagogy: that there is one right way of knowing and doing, that success comes from being superior to others, that one should do whatever it takes to win, that fulfillment is gained by accumulating possessions, that others are too different to relate to, etc. (Howard, 2008).

Why Care About Privileged Children?

There are three distinct reasons to support an affirmative answer to the original question of whether or not we should care about (and, by extension, study) privileged kids' education.

First, if we are to interrupt the reproduction of unequal opportunities and outcomes, we must understand how poverty is not just about poor people but about the relationship between people of all social classes. Focusing only on the marginalized risks making the privileged an "unchanging and unproblematic location" (Bonnett, 1996) or what Brantlinger (2003) refers to as the "unstudied but positively imagined control group against whom Others are favorably compared" (p. 10). In other words, studying privileged students' schooling helps to demystify the assumption that privileged schools are inherently good and in no need of change. Studying "up" as well as "down" thus enriches our understanding of the consequences of privileging/marginalization and how oppression operates.

Second, given that children from privileged communities are very likely to occupy positions of power as they grow older, ensuring that these students are exposed to a critical examination of society and encouraged to orient themselves towards justice is an important (though little understood) strategy in the larger project of interrupting injustice. If not, they risk becoming "misled, miseducated citizens when it comes to sociopolitical and sociohistorical realities" (Gorski, 2006, pp. 165–166). Historically, critically conscious people from dominant groups have had what Freire (2000) called "a fundamental role" (p. 60) in liberation movements. Stories of revolutionary figures from the professional class like Che Guevara and Mohandas Gandhi or White civil rights activists like the abolitionist

Grimke sisters and Freedom Rider Jim Zwerg exemplify the ways in which social capital and power granted to people through unjust systems can be wielded on behalf of groups working to upend them.[7] More cautionary tales, like those of middle-class White feminists marginalizing working-class women and women of color (Thompson, 2002), underscore the importance of caring about the education of privileged students as part of a larger strategic move to create a more just and humane society for all people.

It is important to note (and will be addressed in more depth later) that students are unlikely to come to the same conclusions about how to solve social problems or whether or not to participate in social justice movements. To demand they do so would be indoctrination and anti-democratic at its very core. To expose students to the realities of an unequal world, to raise questions about how best to address that inequality, and to ask students to think about their complicity and obligations, however, is not beholden to one's political affiliations and critically important for a functioning and healthy democracy.

Last, but not least, an interest in privileged students' education represents a concern for them as participants in oppression given that an unjust society dehumanizes not only the marginalized but also those who benefit from its inequality (Freire, 2000; Luthar, 2003). Though benefiting from oppression clearly manifests itself in increased material and social power for net beneficiaries of privilege, it also significantly hinders people's ability to build fulfilling lives (Choules, 2007) and frequently produces feelings of alienation, meaninglessness, randomness, isolation, pain, and dysfunction (McLaren, 1998; Goodman, 2000b; Derman-Sparks & Ramsey, 2006; Denis-McKay, 2007). According to Wise's (2008) memoir of Whiteness,

> To define yourself, ultimately, by what you're not, is a pathetic and heart-breaking thing. It is to stand denuded before a culture that has stolen your birthright, or rather, convinced you to give it up. And the costs are formidable, beginning with the emptiness whites so often feel when confronted by multiculturalism and the connectedness of people of color to their various heritages. That emptiness then gets filled up by the privileges and ultimately forces us to become dependent on them. It's hard to deny that at the end of the day, this self-imposed cultural genocide has cost us more, in the long run, than it's worth.
>
> *(p. 171)*

In addition to these more philosophical concerns, there are tangible physical and mental health issues that may be unique to communities of privilege. This includes higher rates of drug-induced deaths, binge drinking, and suicide (for which the only group with higher rates are Native American men) (Centers for Disease Control and Prevention [CDC] Report, 2011), as well as lower levels of happiness than their less affluent peers, and particular forms of anxiety, depression, and drug use (Luthar, 2003; Levine, 2008). For those committed to the principles of a critical, democratic, social justice education, our compassion and concern should thus include the psychological, social, moral/spiritual, intellectual, material/physical, and societal costs of injustice for privileged youth (Goodman, 2000b).

Ultimately, if we care about social justice and we believe that schooling can help transform society, then we should care about how students of privilege are educated. Examining privileged students' experiences with schooling can help to illuminate how inequality persists, de-normalize elite education, generate strategies for including these people in social movements working towards justice, and to elicit compassion for the ways in which systems of oppression ultimately dehumanize even those they advantage. Deciding to care, of course is only the first step. We now turn to another vexing question: How should these students be educated?

2

DISCONNECTED, PARALYZED, AND CHARITABLE

Social Justice Pedagogy with Privileged Children

> A lot of my students have cultural capital and most of their families are doing pretty well economically. I'm therefore trying to look at the way I teach about social justice issues and see if I am enabling students to use knowledge about oppression to their own advantage rather than take it permanently into their hearts.
>
> *(Paul, a teacher in North's study; North, 2009, p. 165)*

There are many ways to think about how students in privileged communities ought to be educated. One approach that no doubt drives many parents' decisions about where to enroll their children is to think about which school will best prepare them for prestigious universities and job opportunities. In many ways, this is understandable: most parents want their children to have access to a high-quality education and successful futures. Yet only considering how best to prepare students for universities or jobs does little more than preserve, if not enhance, the forces that privilege elite students (Swift, 2003).

Another way to think about the question of how we should educate privileged children (or any children, for that matter) is to consider the needs of a democracy. What kind of citizens and community members do we want and need privileged people to be? What kind of education will best prepare them for embracing these responsibilities? These are loaded questions with inherent normative qualities (What is best? What ought to be?), as well as a range of possible and legitimate solutions. In their influential examination of ten civic educational programs in the United States, Westheimer & Kahne (2004) highlight how educators' pedagogical choices reveal three very different visions that are helpful here of what kinds of citizens are needed for a healthy democracy. These perspectives include *personally responsible citizenship*, *participatory citizenship*, and *justice-oriented citizenship*.

Civic education embracing the perspective of personally responsible citizenship teaches students that the cultivation of citizens with good moral character who demonstrate responsibility, independence, and obedience will solve social problems. Programs promoting participatory citizenship, on the other hand, emphasize taking an active leadership role within established community structures that serve the "less fortunate" in order to improve society. Lastly, educational efforts rooted in justice-oriented citizenship teach students that good citizens question the status quo when it is shown to repeatedly reproduce injustice and actively work to change those established systems through social movements.

Westheimer and Kahne (2004) assert that, though there is some overlap among them, these three approaches present "conflicting priorities." They critique the many civic educational programs rooted in personally responsible or participatory forms of citizenship with the claim that both visions dangerously depoliticize democracy by emphasizing individual, idiosyncratic acts of kindness over social action in the pursuit of justice and encouraging docility over demands for change. Though they acknowledge that both personally responsible and participatory citizens make good community members, they found that attempts to educate students with these ends in mind are not sufficient for a robust democracy. Ultimately, Westheimer and Kahne (2004) call for democratic educational programs that emphasize justice-oriented conceptions of citizenship linked to civic participation, a type of teaching and learning that is also known as social justice pedagogy.

Social Justice Pedagogy

It is easy to become overwhelmed with the multiple educational traditions that intersect and borrow from each other in an attempt to cultivate this kind of justice-oriented citizenship: *anti-oppressive education* (Kumashiro, 2004), *critical pedagogy* (Shor, 1992; McLaren, 1998; Darder, Torres, & Baltodano, 2002; Apple, Au, & Gandin, 2009), *democratic schooling* (Westheimer & Kahne, 1998; Apple & Beane, 2000; Parker, 2003), *equity pedagogy* (McGee & Banks, 1995), *multicultural/anti-racist education* (Nieto, 2000; Banks & Banks, 2006; Sleeter & Grant, 2007; Pollock, 2008), *teaching to transgress* (hooks, 1994), *teaching for equity and justice* (Bigelow, Harvey, Karp, & Miller, 2000), and *teaching for social action* (Schultz, 2008). What these distinct yet interrelated conceptions share are the fundamental principles and objectives within a framework of *social justice education* (Adams, Bell, & Griffin, 1997; Ayers, Hunt, & Quinn, 1998; Banks, 2004).

The working definition for social justice education that is perhaps most useful here is one that attempts to incorporate many of the aforementioned traditions. Chubbuck and Zembylas (2008) cast a wide net when they define it as

> A teacher's effort to transform policies and enact pedagogies that improve the learning and life opportunities of typically underserved students while

equipping and empowering them to work for a more socially just society themselves. This composite definition includes intrapersonal development in the teacher, pedagogy and dispositions that support equitable access to learning for all, a curriculum that can empower all students to become agents of social justice themselves, and activist teachers engaged in challenging and transforming inequitable structures and policies in schools and society.

(p. 285)

This approach can trace its roots to myriad influences: Jesuit priests working within a liberation theological framework, critical theorists working within the Frankfurt School tradition, and popular educators like Paolo Freire working within a "pedagogy of the oppressed"—all actors who mobilized scholarship and education as a means to fight against the deep social and economic inequalities in their communities.

It is worth noting that any conception of social justice education means very little if not linked with the rich philosophical tradition of normative theory exploring why we should value equality and justice and what a society that values equality and justice should look like (e.g., Leistyna & Woodrum, 1996; Fraser, 1997; Gutmann & Thompson, 2004). Hopefully, the following description will appease readers whose visions may differ in important and reasonable ways. In brief, my conception of the "more just world" towards which education ought to orient itself is one that recognizes and affirms difference (e.g., cultural, sexual, political) while maintaining a commitment to fundamental human rights and democratic principles (e.g., freedom of speech and freedom of religion). It is also one that challenges the current distribution of resources in order to secure the basic needs required for human flourishing (e.g., safety, food, shelter, water, love) (Nussbaum, 1992; Fraser, 1997).

I recognize that this description is loaded with loaded terms; indeed, shelves full of books have been written to think through the finer points and inherent tensions in what is meant by "human flourishing," "democratic principles," and "human rights." To be as transparent as possible, my understanding of a more just world is rooted in a critical theoretical framework that assumes unequal power relationships and challenges the belief systems and social relations that (re)produce power differentials. Ultimately, this understanding of a more just world asks what sorts of transformation are needed to eliminate oppression and exploitation. "This question implies not simply an explanatory agenda about the mechanisms that generate economic inequalities," Wright (2008) says, "but a normative judgment about those inequalities—are forms of oppression and exploitation—and a normative vision of the transformation of those inequalities as part of a political project of emancipatory social change" (p. 334).

Butin (2002) wonders if unequal conditions can ever be overthrown given that oppressive structures seem to be so deeply embedded in society that they are immutable and inevitable. In his mind, the goal of social justice pedagogy for privileged people is "not a resistance of and escape from 'oppression', we are all constructed within and constructive of relations of power. The goal is rather the productive use of such power relations, with 'productive' understood as providing greater rather than fewer potentialities to remake oneself" (pp. 14–15). Goodman (2000b), too, notes that, "we need to provide visions and alternatives that change people's ways of thinking, acting, and behaving. … In this sense, the aim is not to change roles or change who has power but to change the very nature of the system" (pp. 195–196). I find these insights helpful and quite pragmatic in that they ask privileged people to think about how best to mobilize their resources in order to build a more just world. For while it is unlikely that privileged students would or could extract themselves entirely from the contexts that privilege them, it is possible to imagine an education that asks them to think about what kind of society they want and what that vision requires of them in their current positions. We must keep in mind however, that while radical social transformation may not be the most immediate or viable of goals, it is one that social justice pedagogy demands educators and their students consider (particularly if they are privileged).

In order to address such issues in a meaningful way, a social justice pedagogical framework relies on three primary tenets: 1) exposing students to multiple perspectives that include the voices of marginalized peoples, 2) a democratic class-room structure that values student voice, and 3) opportunities to participate in project-based learning and community-based social action that address issues of injustice.[1] There are several helpful frameworks mapping out the key elements of such a classroom. Hackman (2005), for instance, identifies five "essential com-ponents": (a) *content mastery* that includes exposure to multiple perspectives, (b) *critical analysis tools* that allow students to question such information, (c) *social change tools* that help prevent students from becoming hopeless or complacent by engaging them in action, (d) *self-reflection tools* for both students and teachers to make sense of their lives within this framework, and (e) an *awareness of multi-cultural group dynamics* that affects how social justice teachers approach the previ-ous four dynamics within a diverse groups of students.

More recently, and quite usefully, North (2009) outlines five "literacies" derived from her study of a working group of teachers struggling with what it means to be engaged in social justice pedagogy. She emphasizes that none of the literacies alone are sufficient but rather must work in concert with and inform each other. The first is a *functional literacy* drawing upon the work of Ladson-Billings (1994) and Delpit (1995) that might be likened to Young's (2008) conception of "powerful knowledge": exposure to information and skills from the dominant culture that translates into access to more opportunities. This kind of literacy is not enough, however; students must also engage in *critical literacy* practices that enable them to examine these skills and knowledge from multiple perspectives (Gutstein, 2006).

According to North (2009), this age-old debate between critical and functional literacies does not, however,

> Adequately capture the development of additional competencies for social justice that require more than a bundle of knowledge and skills. These competencies include cultivating solidarity, working through difficult emotions (like shame, fear, and guilt), and publicly acting up—that is, directly challenging the status quo—when called for. Deep-seated dispositions toward social justice rarely if ever emerge from the efficient, scientific planning of people. ... Instead, poignant experiences and interpersonal relationships often incite people to work collectively for a more just and peaceful world.
>
> *(p. 75)*

Keeping in mind Noddings' (1984) "ethics of care" and Antrop-González & de Jesús' (2006) "critical care," North (2009) thus recommends the concurrent development of a *relational literacy*. She notes, however, that, "even an education that develops critically enlightened and caring citizens does not always realize vibrant, just democratic communities. We also need communication skills that allow us to expose and address conflict and controversial issues nonviolently" (p. 109). Building upon the work of Westheimer and Kahne (2002) and Parker (2003), she establishes the need for just such a *democratic literacy*. Finally, inspired by the work of Greene (1995), she calls for a *visionary literacy* that asks students to practice imagining a better world. This literacy relies heavily upon the arts and students' creative faculties to complement the analytic, rational modes of thinking emphasized by functional and critical literacies.

In summary, social justice pedagogy attends to the following three elements:

1)   a curriculum that includes multiple perspectives (*content mastery/functional and critical literacy*) grounded in an assumption that systemic, institutional oppression exists (*critical analysis tools/critical literacy*);
2)   a democratic classroom where students' voices are valued and lives reflected (*awareness of multicultural dynamics/democratic literacy*) with opportunities to engage in individual critical self-reflection (*awareness of multicultural dynamics/self-reflection tools/relational literacy*); and
3)   practice participating in collective action at the micro and macro levels (*social change tools/democratic and relational literacy*) in order to build a less oppressive society (*social change tools/visionary literacy*).

The hoped-for short- and long-term outcomes of this pedagogy are that students will (a) be aware of injustice in the world and understand its root causes, (b) feel empowered to address that inequity as agents of change, and (c) ultimately act in ways that help to create a more just and equitable world (Ayers, Quinn, & Stovall, 2009).

Complications

In recent years, resources for K-12 classroom teachers engaging in "social justice pedagogy" have become more widespread and accessible (e.g., readers like Ayers, Quinn, & Stovall's *Handbook of Social Justice in Education* (2009), publications from *Rethinking Schools*, grassroots teacher organizations like NYCoRE, curriculum conferences in many major cities, and teacher education programs with "social justice" in their mission). The ubiquity of the term, however, should not imply a unified conception of its meaning, its form, its efficacy, or its goals. Rather, the increased attention to this approach to education raises important questions and exposes tensions with no obvious answers or easy solutions.[2] For example, how should this pedagogy be enacted? Is "teaching for social justice" a process, a goal, or both (Bell, 1997)? How might teachers focus on increasing opportunities for marginalized students by connecting a rigorous curriculum to students' cultures (Ladson-Billings, 1994; Delpit, 1995) while also promoting anti-oppression activism through an inclusive, anti-racist, critical curriculum (Apple, 1993; Ayers, et al., 1998; Apple & Beane, 2000; Freire, 2000; Wade, 2001; Kumashiro, 2004; Au, Bigelow, & Karp, 2007; Anyon, 2009)?

Beyond how teachers should engage in social justice pedagogy, it is also unclear to what ends it should be done: is "justice" about redistribution, recognition, or a more sophisticated relationship between the two (Young, 1990; Fraser, 1997; Gewirtz, 1998; North, 2006)? Should justice-oriented discourse be one of charity, human rights, or privilege (Choules, 2007)? What keeps this pedagogy from being Leftist ideological indoctrination or another form of oppression (Ellsworth, 1989; Butin, 2002; Au, et al., 2007; Applebaum, 2009)? Should "justice" goals focus more on individuals' orientations and actions, present and future, or on the orientations and actions taken as members of a collective society (Westheimer & Kahne, 2004; Gorski, 2006; North, 2008; Leonardo, 2009)? Finally, how might teachers invest in creating counter-hegemonic classrooms while also organizing against inequitable policies at the school, district, state, and national levels (Anyon, 2005; Hackman, 2005; North, 2006)?

Complicating this already sophisticated approach to teaching is that it is attempting to counter the current market-based, managerial common sense promoted by a loose affiliation of neoconservatives, neoliberals, authoritarian populists, and the professional new middle class (Apple, 2006). What results from such a hegemonic force is a national obsession with closing the infamous achievement gap and the creation of policies deleteriously affecting urban schools that primarily serve immigrants, working-class kids, and students of color.[3] These well-documented, increasingly burdensome bureaucratic requirements and pressures on teachers in the public schools seem to render social justice pedagogy a utopian dream (Meiers & Wood, 2004). In addition, some of the successes of integrating a critical, multicutlural, social justice pedagogy into schools have either been co-opted into a "rightist multiculturalism" (Buras, 2008) or banished from districts, as exemplified by recent legislation in Arizona against ethnic studies programs (Orozco, 2012) and the opposition to teaching "critical thinking skills" as part of the GOP party platform in Texas (Republican Party of Texas, 2012).[4]

Despite the overwhelming odds, however, many narratives exist of teachers finding ways to both satisfy and critique the demands of an audit culture without sacrificing their commitment to engaging in content that values multiple and marginalized perspectives, student-centered practices, and democratic social action working with students and the larger community to address social injustice (see Ayers, et al., 1998; Apple & Beane, 2000; Wade, 2001; Gutstein, 2003; Hackman, 2005; North, 2009). A largely anecdotal body of evidence about social justice pedagogy paints a picture of students, teachers, and community members engaged in academically rigorous, personally satisfying, and socially transformative teaching and learning (see Ayers, et al., 1998; Apple & Beane, 2000; Gutstein, 2006; Au et al., 2007; Schultz, 2008; Ayers, et al., 2009; North, 2009). I cannot state clearly enough that, while most public school teachers face standardizing curriculum, larger class sizes, fewer resources, more narrow conceptions of accountability, less autonomy, and stiffer penalties for "failure" (a depressing state of affairs if ever there was one), such a climate does not make social justice pedagogy impossible. If anything, it cries out for a deeper commitment to teaching that critically analyzes society, connects to students' lives, and urges students to act on what they learn.

It is worth noting here that some scholars bemoan the slippery vagueness of the term "social justice" and warn of its becoming an irreversibly empty buzzword despite its proponents' best intentions (Hernández-Sheets, 2003; Hackman, 2005; North, 2006; Chubbuck & Zembylas, 2008; Boyles, Carusi, & Attick, 2009). Its dilution is not only confusing and frustrating to those who align themselves with the tradition, but is potentially counterproductive to the aims most social justice educators promote by asking too little of those in power (Choules, 2007; Leonardo, 2009). Butin (2007), for example, draws attention to how such watered-down definitions tend to serve those who would find it most unpalatable by avoiding the "very difficulty originally meant to be engaged" (p. 2). From a postmodern perspective, Ellsworth (1989) critiques the vagueness of social justice (and its cousin "empowerment") as ahistorical and depoliticized. Using a more critical theoretical lens, Hackman (2005) recognizes the benefit of multiple entry points created by a broad definitional range, but concludes that dilution "ultimately does the field a disservice by … weakening the call for teachers, schools, and communities to be true vanguards for change" (p. 103). Gorski (2006) and Buras (2008) go further in suggesting that this vagueness leaves too much room for Rightist interpretations that purposefully maintain the status quo of inequity (e.g., Hirsch, 1988; Payne, 1996).

Loosely defined and disconnected from its roots, then, it is suggested that perhaps social justice pedagogy should be retired from the educational community's evolving lexicon. While I acknowledge these concerns, I believe the term has a history and potential too rich to be set aside just yet.[5] Ultimately, the tensions surfaced in researcher and practitioner debates about its possible and desirable meanings, though not conclusive, have been quite productive and important (e.g., North, 2006; Chubbuck & Zembylas, 2008).

Social Justice Pedagogy with Privileged Children

With roots firmly planted in traditions of liberation movements with oppressed peoples, the fact that the vast majority of these accounts focus on the possibilities of social justice pedagogy with students from marginalized groups makes historical, even ethical, sense (Giroux, 1992; Au, 2009; Erickson, 2009). Given that privileged children are unlikely to enter schools with a critical consciousness already formed, however, a handful of scholars advocate for the theorization and implementation of social justice pedagogy that is attuned to their unique needs. Denis-McKay (2007) notes that, "because the dominant culture relies on unquestioned privilege, the opportunities to name, critically reflect, and act are equally denied the privileged and the other" (p. 27). According to North (2008), "when some students are struggling to find food and shelter while others are debating the merits of this advanced placement class over that one, we cannot expect a single approach to social justice education to be effective for all students in all contexts." She continues: "We can conclude that those students with the most privileges need to do more than 'learn about' other people's suffering if they are going to effect real social change" (p. 1200).

In terms of race, Leonardo (2009) similarly notes a need for a different approach with White students when he references Lenin's belief that the proletariat must be *educated* while the bourgeoisie *revolutionized*. In addition, he contests the assumption that conventional schools benefit mono-discoursal White students when compared with students of color who are often, by default, immersed in "counter-discourses" and "unofficial" alternative knowledge: "By contrast, white subjects do not forge these same counter-hegemonic racial understandings because their lives also depend on a certain development, that is, color-blind strategies that maintain their supremacy as a group" (p. 83).

And though they explicitly reference "typically under-served youth" as the targeted population for social justice pedagogy, Chubbuck and Zembylas (2008) call for educators and scholars to think about the ways in which

> All students, whether marginalized or from the dominant culture, need to learn and respond to the demands of both recognition and redistribution as expressions of justice. ... In socially just teaching, marginalized students who have been positioned as objects of societal injustice ... are to be empowered to act as subjects who challenge inequitable status quo and work to create a better society [while] ... those students who are part of the

dominant culture also can learn of injustice and embrace their own role as allies in the creation of a more just society.

(pp. 282, 285)

Such attention to group dynamics and the social context of students' lives is surely good practice for all teachers (Hackman, 2005), though it may be particularly salient when considering these implications within a classroom implementing a social justice framework.

Frustratingly, there are few empirical studies that specifically address teachers engaged in social justice pedagogy with privileged K-12 students (Hernández-Sheets, 2003; Curry-Stevens, 2007). Those that do exist tend to focus on a critique of service-learning with privileged students (e.g., Wade, 2001; Himley, 2004; Gorski, 2006; Butin, 2007; Swaminathan, 2007), a description of multicultural education with White students in undergraduate classes (e.g., Garmon, 2004; Chizhik & Chizhik, 2005), an examination of privileged people's discourses around privilege (e.g., Choules, 2007), or an analysis of adult learners from privileged groups (e.g., Goodman, 2000a, 2000b; Manglitz, 2003; Curry-Stevens, 2007; Heinze, 2008). The majority of existing literature that connects social justice pedagogy with non-marginalized populations focuses on White, middle-class, pre-service teacher-education students considered to be the "first significant audience" of social justice pedagogy (Chubbuck & Zembylas, 2008) as they learn how to teach students of color and/or students from high-poverty urban communities (e.g., Cochran-Smith, 2004; Garmon, 2004; McDonald & Zeichner, 2009; Zeichner & Flessner, 2009).

In the late 1960s, Miel and Kiester (1967) conducted a study of suburban schools showing a need for the curriculum to include challenging social issues to expand affluent children's "life-space." Twenty years later, Howard (1981) advocated a "multiethnic curriculum for monoethnic schools" with Project REACH (Rural Education and Cultural Heritage), a four-phase curriculum framework focused on human relations, cultural/ethnic self-awareness, multicultural/multi-ethnic awareness, and cross-cultural experiences. Building upon his work, Peoples-Wessinger (1994) also wrote about her time as a physical-education teacher exploring multicultural education in a monocultural (White) school in Vermont. Examples of more recent work include Derman-Sparks and Ramsey's (2006) book *What If All the Kids Are White?*, which offers research reviews, case-study vignettes, and voices of teachers in the field in their guide to anti-bias/multicultural early childhood education of White children. Drawing upon the literature of adolescent psychology, Seider (2008, 2009) identifies a decrease in affluent students' levels of empathy for economically disadvantaged people after participation in a social justice pedagogy English class. And Denis-McKay (2007), a teacher-researcher working at an international school in Mali, explicitly focuses on the social justice teaching and learning of K-12 privileged youth in theorizing about how her project-based curriculum brought students into joint cultural production with a local group of people native to the region. Additionally, teachers have published articles in *Rethinking Schools* reflecting on their attempts at social justice pedagogy with affluent and suburban students (e.g., Frewing, 2001; Staples, 2005).

When read together, this literature points to three common reactions of privileged children when exposed to social justice pedagogy. First, though they may well learn of injustices in the world, privileged students are likely to frame these issues as abstract and demonstrate a deep unawareness of their root causes. Second, whereas marginalized students may come to feel empowered by learning about systemic oppression, privileged students are likely to feel overwhelmed by guilt or anger and resist this pedagogy. Third, if students choose to participate in social action as a result of their exposure to social justice pedagogy, privileged students are more likely to act in ways that frame themselves as savior figures who help a deficit "Other" in a patronizing or superficial way. Instead of expanding their worldview, empowering them to act, and engaging them in action as social justice pedagogues hope, the literature ultimately warns of the potential for social justice pedagogy with privileged students to backfire. What follows is a deeper examination of each of these unintended consequences in terms of awareness, empowerment, and action.

Awareness

It is unlikely that students from communities of privilege will have had much explicit exposure in their lives to the counter-hegemonic content at the heart of social justice pedagogy, though they are, of course, living it every day. Because privilege is primarily "learned" by absorbing messages through exposure to media, interactions with significant people in their lives, and growing up in communities physically isolated from people different from them, privileged youth tend to be sheltered by forces rendered invisible to them (Derman-Sparks & Ramsey, 2006). Included in their lessons is the most important message of all: to preserve an aura of inevitability about their privileges. This "invisibilizing" need not be of malicious intent to function (Curry-Stevens, 2007).[6] For example, it is not uncommon for White people to avoid talking explicitly about race—what Pollock (2004) calls being "colormute." Race in such situations, however, is playing a deeply important role as an invisible presence; it "never comes up" simply because people are actively avoiding it—not because it is irrelevant.

When privileged people do challenge the reproduction of inequalities, it is often only when it serves their needs (e.g., claiming to be "color blind" rather than critically reflecting on race in their lives and the ways in which they are complicit in the reproduction of racist social structures) (Hurtado, 1996; Applebaum, 2010). Delpit (1995) presents the idea that ignorance and awareness likely co-exist within privileged people, that "those with power are frequently least aware of—or least willing to acknowledge—its existence" (p. 24). Of all the metaphors used for privileged students' ignorance of injustice (e.g., "sheltered", "in a bubble"), hers is one of my favorites. She says that privileged individuals (who are privileged, she notes, whether they admit to it or not) have worldviews that "exist in protected cocoons" (p. 74). What I like most about this is the hope that is embedded within it; one is meant to emerge from a cocoon as a stronger and wiser, transformed being meant for broader horizons.

When it comes to thinking about privileged students' capacity to be aware of injustice, Leonardo (2009) quite helpfully distinguishes between racial *understanding* and racial *knowledge*, claiming that most Whites have little of the former and a lot of the latter. This distinction holds for other forms of privilege as well: students from wealthy families, for example, certainly know that poverty exists, but their understanding of how poverty and wealth are intertwined and experienced is likely to be weak at best. Knowledge about injustice can help students keep an abstract, impersonal distance from oppression; it is something that happened "back then" or "over there" to "them." Understanding, on the other hand, requires empathy and a willingness to implicate oneself in the issue at had—a much more difficult task. When exposed to social justice pedagogy, privileged students, then, are likely to focus on knowledge of injustice rather than understanding its root causes and connections to their lives (Howard, 2008) as it is "often easier to deplore [oppression] and its effects than to take responsibility for the privilege some of us receive as a result of it" (Rothenberg, 2002, p. 1).

Even if teachers (or parents) set out to challenge this conception by engaging in social justice pedagogy, privileged students may still find ways to "capitalize" on knowledge of injustice as a way to increase their marketability (Goodman, 2000a). A student may integrate their new knowledge about "diversity" as a way to write a much more attractive college essay, for example, or leverage required community-service hours in order to gain entrance into more competitive universities. Though her study does not focus on privileged students, North (2009) expresses great concern for (and not a little frustration with) these students who incorporate their new critical literacy into what Lareau (2003) calls a "repeated performance of entitled selves" or Khan's (2011) "ease" of the new elite that continues to legitimate the social order. Ultimately, she worries that "teaching students the rules of a social system that already benefits them could have the unintentional effect of strengthening that very system" (p. 126). Social justice educators in communities of privilege thus face a difficult challenge as they struggle against norms of competitive individualism that encourage such interpretations of their pedagogy (Goodman, 2000b).

Empowerment

Because social justice pedagogy asks teachers to expose privileged children to perspectives that often challenge the status quo, few expect these students to jump on the social justice bandwagon as willingly as might those from marginalized groups. Rather than feel empowered by knowledge or understanding of injustice, privileged students are likely to feel confused, angry, or challenged (Rothenberg, 2002), immobilized by guilt (Rodriguez, 2000), or deny complicity in the reproduction of oppressive forms (Applebaum, 2007). "This makes pedagogy for the privileged significantly different from pedagogy of the oppressed," says Curry-Stevens (2007), "where the liberation impact is clear and direct and the process typically marked by ease and freedom and relatively unscathed by resistance and denial. We need to remind ourselves that this form of change engenders resistance" (p. 41). A not-so-subtle frustration with students' opposition to these changes abounds in the literature, positioning students from dominant groups as the most challenging population with which to attempt this work. Again, a note about indoctrination: the opposition I mention here is not in reference to students' diverse and varied perspectives about what ought to be done with regards to their complicity with systems of oppression, but rather about their potential opposition to being asked to think about those issues at all.

Exasperation is tempered, however, with a dose of realism about how difficult it is for people to change their minds about deeply held worldviews and how likely it is that they will experience loss with change (Heinze, 2008). Resistance, then, is neither unexpected nor irrational as the consequences for answering new questions and potentially adopting new beliefs and practices have serious implications for people's lives. I must also highlight the fact that we are thinking about privileged *children*, who, like children born into poverty or to families from marginalized groups, do not come to such a position by choice and have very little culpability in perpetuating oppressive forms themselves (Denis-McKay, 2007). A bit of compassion here is called for. If the hope is that privileged people work to dismantle the systems that unjustly privilege them, then any process working towards such ends is sure to engender a lot of pain, uncertainty, and grief that educators would be wise to acknowledge.

Even if privileged students choose to embrace social justice pedagogy, peers and families may express concern and encourage a resistant response. There is likely little opportunity, support, or incentive within their communities for people from dominant groups to critically explore their identity and examine its social implications (Goodman, 2000b). Initially supportive students may thus revert back to their "original blindness" as the fear generated by examining themselves and the risk of damaging relationships with their social networks appears too great (Heinze, 2008). Ultimately, there is some hope in the literature that students can be persuaded to embrace social justice pedagogy with a patient, supportive teacher at the helm.

Action

Along with hope, the literature offers a healthy dose of skepticism about whether or not the transformation of privileged people's worldviews is actually possible and whether or not such change will ultimately lead them to act in ways that will disrupt oppression. As White studies scholar Tim Wise (2002) admits, "privilege tastes good and we're loath to relinquish it" (p. 108). With regards to race privilege, Berlak and Moyenda (2001) claim that, ultimately, "White people are going to do what they damn well please" (p. 136). Hernández-Sheets (2000) notes that, "the connection from the process of White racial identity development that potentially creates change agents committed to social action to effective pedagogy, is unclear, undocumented, and unrealistic" (p. 19). In fact, attention to race may encourage White students to "create solidarity" in their racial identity rather than work to rearticulate it (Rodriguez, 2000). Privileged people are thus "politically unrelia-ble"; they may change their hearts and minds, but refuse to act on these changes either individually or collectively (Goodman, 2000b; Curry-Stevens, 2007).

For those privileged students who do choose to act, the literature is clear that they should do so as *allies* with oppressed peoples' struggles rather than patroniz-ing or colonizing saviors swooping in to aid the Other (Kivel, 2002; Edwards, 2006). Privileged students can be valuable to social movements, especially with regards to their powerful forms of capital they can mobilize (Goodman, 2000b; Curry-Stevens, 2007). A conception of alliance rather than service can help focus attention on root causes of injustice and long-term solutions. For instance, Wise (2002), urges people from all backgrounds to unite "against their common problem: the mostly white lawmakers who prioritize jails and slashing taxes on the wealthy over meeting the needs of most people" (p. 109) rather than engage in more superficial action addressing only the symptoms of injustice.

These alliances between the privileged and the oppressed, however, cannot come at the expense of the oppressed. An ethos of charity is, frustratingly, a perhaps well-intentioned but all-too common framework in the education of privileged youth that frequently descends into a type of voyeurism or what Hernández-Sheets (2000) calls "helperism" which is "platitudinous and no longer viable" for marginalized peoples (p. 19). Such an approach can be disruptive and distracting when privileged students are briefly dropped into an organization when what is most needed from them is financial support or a commitment to build long-term relationships with a movement over time. Such shallow forms of service learning can obscure underlying causes of injustice, reify privileged norms, excuse privileged students from critically reflecting on their lives, and reproduce a false sense of "Us" and "Them" (Butin, 2007; Choules, 2007).

To avoid this trap, scholars advise privileged people to become involved in social movements not simply to help others but in order to liberate themselves (Denis-McKay, 2007; Wise, 2008). Those who focus on "humanization" warn against demonizing or punishing the privileged, focusing instead on how their privilege can be mobilized to help abolish oppressive structures and conditions (Goodman, 2000b; Heinze, 2008). Though focusing such attention on privileged children may "re-center" them at the expense of marginalized youth (Hernández-Sheets, 2000; Curry-Stevens, 2007), addressing a pedagogy of privileged students rooted in an "analytics of the oppressed" is markedly different than the historic centering of Eurocentric traditions in which privilege itself was immune to critique and transformation (Leonardo, 2009).

With these potential "backfire" responses to the hoped-for goals of social justice pedagogy with privileged children in mind (awareness, agency, and action), I now turn to examining the practices of two teachers working with different groups of privileged students. One taught in a suburban public school, the other at an elite urban private academy. How were their students different? How were they alike? What challenges did students' conceptions of themselves and the world present to these teachers? And, importantly, how did these teachers try to overcome them?

PART II

The Education of Privileged Youth in Practice

3

SHELTERED AND EXCEPTIONAL

Privileged Students' Conceptions of Themselves and Their Communities

> By allowing white America to remain in the bubble of unreality, white privilege
> ultimately distorts our vision, and makes it difficult for us to function as fully
> rational beings. It protects us from some of life's cruelties, and allows us to wander
> around, largely oblivious to the fires that, for others, burn all around them. In the
> end … this bubble of unreality can be a dangerous place to reside.
>
> *(Wise, 2008, p. 60)*

In Part I of this book, I justified why the education of privileged children
ought to be of concern and laid out a theoretical framework to help guide those
interested in such work. In Part II, I now turn to examining what social justice
pedagogy with privileged children looks like in practice. My findings are not from
a large random sample data set from which I can make broad, sweeping claims
about privileged children, the longitudinal effects of social justice pedagogy on
privileged students, or their subsequent impact on the world. Instead, these
two instrumental ethnographic case studies (Stake, 1995) represent my questions
about what social justice pedagogy with privileged youth looks like in practice in
order to provide interested educators with an intimate look at the challenges and
possibilities of this work in the field. Any claims I make are thus intended to
lay the groundwork for future studies and action research projects rather than
inform policy decisions.[1] For those interested in reading more about my research
methodology, please see Appendix B for a more detailed description. A quick
note: all names and identifying characteristics of locations and people have been
changed or omitted to protect their anonymity.

If we are to investigate how best to teach privileged students about social
responsibility within a social justice framework, then how they think of themselves in relation to others becomes an important place to start. This first chapter

of Part II thus focuses on the different ways that students in the suburbs and students in the city conceptualized their communities. The ways in which the suburban students talked about their suburb, for instance, and the ways in which the teacher called them out as privileged reinforced the idea that they were some-how separate from the world living in a paradoxical dystopia/utopia. On the other hand, the primarily upper-class private school students thought of themselves as sophisticated, savvy urban dwellers at ease amidst the diversity and chaos of the city. Ultimately, what emerges is a picture of the suburbs as a "bubble" set apart from the world and the private city school as a peripatetic "enclave" set above the world. I now turn to examining these very different perceptions of community that are at the heart of two very different approaches to social justice pedagogy with privileged students: *bursting the bubble* and *disturbing the comfortable*.[2]

The Suburbs

West Town High School

Suburban West Town is a city in its own right with close to 150,000 residents living between interstates that carry commuters away from urban life. It boasts more miles of streets than its parent city, a feat made possible by aesthetically pleasing (yet perpetually confusing) curving roads and hundreds of tree-lined cul-de-sacs around which sit spacious two-story homes and large, manicured lawns. A few major arteries cut through the suburb to offer up rows of chain box stores, car dealerships, and shopping malls.

The segregating effects of its origins as a haven for "White flight" are clear; less than 20% of the community is constituted of people of color compared with 63% in the city.[3] Two-fifths of this group includes professional-class South and East Asians, engineers and doctors whose children dominate West High's wall of National Merit Scholars. The remaining three-fifths is split evenly between Latino and Black families, most of whom have come to West Town in the past few years after gentrifying efforts in the city drove up rents in previously low-income areas. These students are noticeably invisible in terms of the school's various halls of fame: while East and South Asian students are the majority of National Merit Scholars, White students are the only faces for each year's "Student of the Year" award. Not one Black or Latino student's face appears on either wall.

In contrast with their under-representation in these public forms of recogni-tion, Blacks and Latinos are dramatically over-represented in West Town's poverty rates. Though combined they represent 15% of the population, 28% of families under the poverty level are Black and 15% are Latino. In general, the suburb is solidly upper middle class: only 3.3% of the community falls under the poverty line, the median income for West Town residents is close to $100,000, and the average home value is $400,000.[4] Nearly all of its residents went to high school, two-thirds graduated from college, and close to a quarter of its residents have graduate degrees. Politically, West Town is less conservative than its neighbors, but is still an assumed victory district for Republicans.

In other words, the community is a realtor's dream touting itself with familiar buzzwords: "safe," "beautiful," and "clean" with "excellent schools." Of the several high schools in town, West High is one of the oldest and enjoys positive reputations for its arts, athletics, and academics including an honorable mention in recent *Time* and *Newsweek* lists of "America's best high schools." It boasts more than twenty Adanced Placement (AP) courses and over one hundred extracurricular activities in which more than half of its 3000 students participate. The majority of its two hundred staff members hold Masters degrees. And with a mean score of 25 in the standardized test ACT, 98% of its graduates go on to post-secondary education and most attend four-year universities around the country.[5]

The two-story school building, which sits at the center of a sprawling campus amidst sports fields and parking lots filled with newer models of expensive cars, was constructed in the iconic aesthetic of a mid-century suburban school. Several wings house a large auditorium, gymnasiums, two cafeterias, a media center, art studios, labs, and dozens of classrooms. The main doors are kept locked to the outside during the school day; visitors must buzz to enter and then check in with a friendly staff woman at a welcome center outside of the main office. Every day I visited, she would scan my license to make a temporary ID badge with my photograph and destination printed on the front. Once inside, I would walk through wide, tiled halls lit by overhead fluorescent lights and covered with posters for events and clubs that hung above bright blue lockers. Before classes started and during passing periods, the halls filled with crowds of kids dressed to fit in with discernible cliques beyond which there was little visible diversity: a handful of Black students talked and laughed around an open table, a group of Latino boys in uniform headed to soccer practice, and a few girls wearing hijab linked arms as they gossiped on their way to class, but otherwise the vast majority of students were White.

The Students

After a week of informal observations of his three sections of Urban History, Vernon Sloan introduced me to the class we had chosen for the study and allowed me to make a brief presentation about my work. Of the thirty students in his class, thirteen upperclassmen (seven boys and six girls) returned consent forms (see Table 3.1). Of the thirteen, all but two identified as middle or upper middle class: Xavier identified as being from a working-class family and Patrick identified as only recently and partially upper middle class because of his working-class mother's remarriage to a much wealthier man. All but three students identified as White. Luna told me halfway through the semester that her mom was from Mexico and that few people knew she was "half Hispanic." Mel was the son of immigrant Chinese engineers and Henry was the son of two affluent Black

TABLE 3.1 Vernon Sloan's Students

Student	Race	Economic status	Years in the district	Political affiliation
Brian	White	Upper Middle	Elementary, Middle, High	Undecided
Claire	White	Upper Middle	Elementary, Middle, High	Liberal
Emma	White	Upper Middle	Middle, High	Conservative
Fred	White	Upper Middle	Elementary, Middle, High	Conservative
Henry	Black	Upper Middle	Middle, High	Independent
John	White	Upper Middle	Elementary, Middle, High	Liberal
Jude	White	Upper Middle	Elementary, Middle, High	Liberal
Luna	White	Middle	Middle, High	Undecided
Mel	Asian	Upper Middle	Elementary, Middle, High	Liberal
Patrick	White	Upper Middle	Elementary, Middle, High	Liberal
Taylor	White	Upper Middle	Elementary, Middle, High	Undecided
Teegan	White	Middle	Elementary, Middle, High	Undecided
Xavier	White	Working Class	Elementary, Middle, High	Liberal

businesspeople. All but one of the participating students had attended schools in West Town or the neighboring suburbs since elementary school (Henry had moved in junior high school).

The students signed up to take the class for a variety of reasons. Mel and Patrick were self-described "hipster" artistic rebels who enjoyed Vernon's take on history. Others, like Taylor and Teegan, were quieter girls in class who identified as being on the fringes of more popular crowds and had simply been interested in the course description. Vernon recruited John, a football player, for his reputation as a congenial, smart kid. Super-involved Emma signed up for the class primarily because of her love for the city while many others joined after hearing good things about the field trips. Though a few of the students were friends outside of class, most of them knew each other only by reputation given the large size of the school; they were placed into this particular section of the course not by choice but because of their corresponding class schedules.

Sheltered Students: "It's Not Like the Rest of the World"

When asked to describe their community (West Town and its high school) during our first one-on-one interviews, nearly every student immediately used the word "bubble" in response. This "bubble" was most frequently described as "safe" and was almost universally celebrated as a "great place to raise kids." Said Emma:

> This sounds weird, but I like the way that me and my siblings have turned out. I don't know—sometimes I think, like, "Okay, I kind of, like, want to do exactly what my parents did to make my kids be the same."

The bubble was widely regarded as a place where "nothing bad happened." When asked to give examples of injustice in West Town, for instance, Brian noted that:

> I'm getting the big end of the stick, but it's like I'm not knowing that. It's just natural to me. It's seems like everyone's getting that. But I don't know, like, in West Town—injustice? I don't know any good examples of that in West Town. I feel like everyone's getting a big end here.

Students seemed well aware that growing up in the bubble afforded them certain advantages. For example, Luna was not alone in the way she categorized her education:

> I'm pretty glad I came out of West Town' cause when they're, like, looking at your college transcripts they're gonna take a look at that school and they're gonna be, like, "Oh, West Town High."

Xavier echoed this assessment, but wondered about its veracity and expressed concern for students who were not native to the bubble:

> Someone coming from the outside might not be able to adjust correctly. Like, the standards are higher,' cause, I mean, we talk about how our school or our district is, like, number one in the world and stuff like that.

Occasionally, students expressed a bit of shame or embarrassment about living in the "bubble." Some of this seemed to stem from a frustration about being misrepresented and a belief that people outside of the bubble have the wrong idea about people on the inside. Most of the White, middle- and upper-class students were quick to tell me that West Town was more diverse than its reputation as a "rich, White" place implied. Taylor noted that:

> Whenever I say I'm from West Town, people are, like, "Oh. Stuck-up rich White kid." You know? Even though I think it's pretty diverse—not super diverse, but more diverse than that.

These students did not want to be considered a "dumb uppity suburbanite," in Emma's words. She went on to say:

> You know, people think you're someone who is ignorant of things and completely self-centered and just worried about materialistic things and stuff like that which, I don't know, I feel like you find that everywhere you go and it's just one of those stereotypes that I don't believe in, but I'm still self-conscious about it so I don't tell people where I'm from.

Claire told me candidly that she regretted how "West Town is really beige." She was not alone in her envy of the "worldliness" of city kids compared to the degree with which suburban kids are sheltered:

> Kids in the city are involved in more worldly things. It would be cool to be in their situations because you wouldn't be so one-track minded. People here cry if they get a bad grade and it's not the end of the world. ... When kids from the suburbs go to college, there's, like, a wake-up call when they're going to have to be instantly adults.

Emma, too, expressed concern that this sheltering of suburban residents gave them few chances to develop "character":

> They have their block parties, and they have their soccer moms, their mini vans, their nice schools where they can drop their kids off and pick them up afterwards, and, like, their parks where they can let their kids go play without having to worry about violence or stuff like that. So, like, they're not really negative things, the things I'm describing. Why wouldn't someone want to live here? But then it's, like, I guess there are other things that are more important in shaping someone as a person. Like if you never see poverty, if you never see people who need, like, if you never have the opportunity to help people because everyone already has everything, then maybe your character isn't affected as much? I don't know. Like, if you're ignorant to, like, the bad things, then the good things don't seem as good.

Though it may seem to be a benefit of the bubble, students noted that its "shielding" from the outside world's "cruel realities" may not ultimately be what is best for kids, particularly with regards to preparing to leave the "real world" when they "grow up." According to Xavier,

> The bubble is basically parents trying to shield their kids from the realities, like, the cruel realities of the real world. ... I think there's a lot of kids that grow up here and they're sheltered by their parents' money and, like, for example, if they get in trouble—legal or anything—like, their parents will just pay their way out of it instead of them having to, like, deal with real world situations.

Jude agreed:

> I know a lot of people who have gone through their entire childhood who have never had to do a thing and they are rewarded like they are amazing. And then when they get exposed to the real world, and their parents let go, they didn't know how to handle it and their lives fell apart.

To Henry, West Town is:

> A nice place to grow up, but it's not real. If you go out into the real world, people will look at you and you will get knocked out for it or they just won't give it to you because this is a bubble.

Several students focused on the fact that being within the bubble can warp someone's perception of reality in disturbing ways. Patrick noted that, in the city,

> There is a lot more stuff in front of your eyes. I don't think anyone should be sheltered in any way—a lot of people don't have a choice. There is this quote from a song I love: "My eyes have been pried open and I can't look away." If you live in the city, you can't unlearn stuff that happens. Here, people rationalize that stuff away because they have one Black friend.

In Henry's words,

> Everything here is so nice and kept clean and it's not like the rest of the world. The people that live here—they know what they want and try to keep out what they don't want.

Interestingly, many of the students mentioned "West Town moms" as the worst offenders of trying to create an artificial reality in the bubble as a way to shelter their children.[6] According to Taylor, West Town is

> Filled with a lot of giant houses with moms who are worried about everything, getting all flustered about the slightest changes. They're uptight and rich. It's not what I want it to be.

The most frequent example students gave for how people in the bubble consciously try to create an illusion of perfection regarded the city's treatment of a rather infamous homeless man in town. According to Jude,

> I keep asking questions about him and I get the impression that people are uncomfortable by the poverty of others.

Luna similarly noted:

> We want to maintain this image as like a West Town suburbia like, "Oh, we don't have homeless. Oh, it's not a problem here," you know? But, like, you have to open your eyes and, like, see that it's there. We want to maintain the image that there are no problems so we try to, like, hide it, so basically

we want it to be, like, there are no problems so we try to get rid of the problems, to try to hide them, but at the same time get rid of them.

Students of color and from the working class were more consistent critics of the bubble. Mel, for example, was just beginning to articulate how uncomfortable he felt because of his "difference" as a person of color despite his family's upper-middle-class status. When asked about growing up in West Town, he remembered:

> I think back to all the kids' mothers who were friends and who arranged play dates that I was not invited to. I think there are certain kids who I will never be friends with because I am not up to their par—whose mothers have maids to clean the house, who like to decorate and volunteer. My mom was never one of those moms. Being an immigrant, people always have to ask twice what she is saying. You never realize these things until you're older, why you feel the way you do. All the kids that have befriended me are misfit kids who went through a lot more crap. They were more down-to-earth and less disillusioned by what life should be. This leads me to believe that I may forever be hanging out with more mediocre, but more real, people who may not be making as much money—just hanging out where everything smells like smoke and the floors are dirty. If that's where I have always felt like that's where I belong, then it's hard to believe that I will ever be a part of the upper middle class.

Henry, the only Black student in class, exposed a similar feeling of Otherness when I asked him to give advice to students coming to West Town.

> I would say don't change yourself for people, just be yourself and try to fit in where you fit in,' cause people—even if you're, like, from some other country, you'll still be able to be friends with other people because they're accepting around here. Sometimes they'll make little jokes, say snide remarks. But that just comes with the territory, just living life. I don't really care too much about what people think. … [Katy: How do you think you got to be like that—to just not care about]' Cause I live around predominantly White people that just—you know, White people just say what's on their mind and I just have to deal with it because that's the way real life is. And if I cared about every single thing, I would probably be really angry all the time and be upset about every little thing. But there's no use in trying to do that.

When asked about fitting in at school, Xavier, the only student who identified himself as being from a working-class background, noted that:

> In West Town, specifically, there's an injustice in, like, the bar is set so high that, like, people think that it's easy because they are already above

the bar. Like, people expect everyone to be above the bar and they don't understand how hard it actually is to, like, get up to that point. They're just born into that so they don't really understand the working class so much and what it is like to work long hours for low wages. Just, like, being here you have a lot more privilege than a lot of the world but seeing like my difference in privilege than other people who are more affluent has influenced me. ... I just see the standard as unrealistic so I don't really follow it. I feel empathy for people on the other side who are struggling.

In addition, he was one of the only White students to explicitly address racism in West Town:

Because this is a sheltered community, there's problems with race and stuff. People don't understand what it's like. I remember my freshman year, like, I had never even met Sloan and I was in the hallway and people were telling jokes—racial jokes, like Black jokes. Sloan called us in, I was just listening, and he called this whole group of people into the room and gave them a giant lecture of what it's like to be Black in West Town and how like it's a completely different cultural difference and they're so out of their element. I never thought of it that way before, how hard it must be for them to try to live in West Town.

In general, most of the students described positive attributes of the bubble with more than a little pride and gratitude with an awareness that having been educated in West Town will serve them well in the future in terms of college and job opportunities. As they used it, the "bubble" in which the suburban students lived was particularly good at keeping out undesirable elements as a means to maintaining order and cultivating a lifestyle that was more comfortable than other places with much harsher realities. They framed the bubble as a place where injustice was made invisible, the voices of those suffering muffled. It seemed that few people in the bubble were aware of, or curious about, issues of injustice in their community and the world.

Students thus described themselves as sheltered and, though they expressed gratitude for certain aspects of this sheltering (namely its comfort and safety), they ultimately felt frustrated by not being more "exposed" to the "real" world. Overall, the students (and especially those who were White and from the middle/ upper class) characterized living "in the bubble" the following ways: 1) there are many good things in the suburbs that anyone would want (primarily safety, "good schools", and cleanliness); 2) the bubble is more complex than its reputa-tion may imply; 3) bubble residents are separate from the "real world;" and 4) ultimately, this sheltering has undesirable consequences and is a potential source of shame for students.

In the Bubble

Given this perception of their community, it is important to think through what it means to perceive of one's life as in a "bubble." What was perhaps most striking in their descriptions was how articulate the students were about the ways in which the bubble combined utopian and dystopian elements. Vernon, too, expressed an awareness of this tension when he asked the students one day: "How do you help the poor underclass into an idyllic world while, on the other hand, maybe this world isn't idyllic?" In his assessment of the suburbs, British cultural studies scholar David Chaney (1997) contends that:

> While it may be trivializing the reference to describe suburbs as utopian places, I think it is appropriate to see them as harbouring utopian aspirations. … Of course, one can point out that this vision is sustained by precise social differentiations between suburban districts, and powerful mythologies of ever-intensifying dangers of social breakdown articulated in frightening narratives of urban disintegration, criminal and particularly racial violence and social parasitism. … The positive vision of the polite community is therefore dependent upon complementary nightmare visions of impolite disrespect.
>
> *(pp. 139–140)*

Chaney (1997) ultimately describes suburbs as contradictory places whose residents are in constant search of "romantic intimations of authenticity in the midst of conformity" (p. 146). He and the students understand that the "bubble" can only exist in relation to an "Other" outside world that is perceived as simultaneously more authentic and more dangerous. Though they appreciated the safety and security of their "bubble" world, students' desire for "real" lives and "authentic" experiences was quite powerful.

Beyond the philosophical paradox of a dystopia/utopia, other research indicates that even the physical nature of suburbs (long driveways, large yards, little public transportation) quite literally keeps their residents set apart from the world and each other (Wilson-Doenges, 2000). As Pattillo (2008) notes in her description of social class as a production of people living in neighborhoods, "boundary maintenance is a mainstay of middle class community organizing" (p. 266). The "bubble" for these students, therefore, is not simply a metaphor but a literal manifestation of the suburban desire to draw clear boundaries that isolate them from those considered dangerous or less deserving. Thus, these students see themselves as living *apart from* the world, as separate from those living "real" lives.

While bubbles protect and preserve what they contain, they inevitably warp the perspective of those inside, given the domed, convex nature of their enclosure. If you look out, the image will be distorted like a funhouse mirror, if you can see the image at all. The sounds on the other side of the bubble are much harder to hear, if you can hear them at all. In addition to this obliviousness, your home is positioned as "artificial" (it is as inauthentic and unnatural as a greenhouse is when compared with a rainforest) and what is outside the bubble is subsequently positioned as "real." Rather than seen as a place deeply connected in historical, political, cultural, and economic ways to the rest of humanity, then, the bubble is dangerously framed as an apolitical haven from the "real world."

Though this divorce from the "real world" may have garnered benefits for its residents, it has also meant a great loss in terms of cultural and intrapersonal resources that prevents relationships from developing between those on either side of the bubble's wall (or, on some level, within it). For instance, many students mentioned how "bland" and "boring" their middle class, suburban existence was compared with the lives they envisioned of their peers in the city. Especially after field trips into the city, students talked about feeling as if their community was "sterile" and "lifeless." In Luthar's (2003) review of psychological research investigating the experiences of suburban residents, he notes that modern living

> Presents relatively few threats to physical well-being.... Ironically, therefore, the greater the availability of amenities of modern living in a community, the fewer are the occurrences of critical events that indicate to people which of their friends are truly engaged in their welfare and which are only fair-weather companions.... In essence, therefore, the rich are the least likely to experience the security of deep social connectedness that is routinely enjoyed by people in communities where mutual dependence is unavoidable (Myers, 2000a).
>
> *(p. 1585)*

Indeed, the luxury of choice and autonomy associated with the suburbs can lead to depression and a lack of intimacy (Schwartz, 2000).

Bursting the Bubble

As a consequence, the task of social justice pedagogy with these students seems to be about highlighting the ways their lives are inextricably connected, both to people outside and within the suburbs, and examining the ways in which the bubble is an illusion. When asked about his vision of social justice pedagogy, Vernon correspondingly described a need for students to "cross the line" that divides the rich from poor and Black from White. On many occasions he referenced Jonathan Kozol who, according to Vernon,

> Talked about that artificial line that separates the poor from the affluent that the media presents us, this image of poverty being bad and then the people are bad so we have to protect ourselves. That goes back to the White flight of the 50s and the sociological models like the "toilet syndrome,"

Philip Slater's idea that we build porcelain highways out of the problems we have developed, so we separate our children and ignore the problems of the city. You have to cross that line. If you don't, then how else are you able to see it? So, maybe a porch isn't a good an analogy—stepping out into the yard, or at least being a part of it so that you can know that there is a place that you can go safely.

Most frequently, Vernon called his teaching an attempt to "burst the bubble." It was a philosophy he discussed not only with me, but also in class with his students, asking them to confront the border of that protective cocoon and, ultimately, to cross over it. This vivid metaphor meshed with his students' conception of one urban world from which come authentic truth and wisdom, and one suburban world that is sheltered and sterile.

A significant challenge for Vernon within this framework of "bursting the bubble" lay in addressing issues of injustice without exoticizing Others, romanticizing their plight, or reifying deficit stereotypes. It was quite easy for students stepping out of the bubble for the first time to veer into non-critical terrain such as color blindness (See? The kids in the ghetto are just like you and me!) or patronizing charity (Those poor kids in the ghetto—I am so lucky! I should help them!) as they reject fear of or apathy about Others. The authentic/inauthentic binary he so often referenced and in which the kids believed they lived was problematic as an analytic frame rather than the object of analysis. Students were in need of a scaffolded, critical analysis of the bubble as a human-made, socio-historical construction with deep connections to the real suffering and thriving outside of it.

The City

Kent Academy

In contrast to the spacious, green appeal of the West Town "bubble," the Upper North neighborhood in the heart of the city is a dense amalgamation of turn-of-the-century three- and four-story brick buildings hovering over one-way streets. Flowering trees peek out from behind the wrought-iron gates of row-house gardens and evenly spaced bricked enclosures in the cobblestones. Both sides of the side streets are filled with parked cars (mostly new luxury models) and daytime pedestrians (frequently women of color pushing the strollers of White children). The main arteries cutting through the neighborhood are filled with boutiques, general shopping, and restaurants. This area had been home to a variety of immigrant groups until gentrification policies and calculating realtors forced them out in the late 1980s by luring de-ethnicized professional-class Whites from the suburbs with the promise of a "safe" city neighborhood near downtown businesses and attractions. After pushback from earlier residents prompted the creation of low-income housing in the area, construction of gated townhouses for the newcomers began almost immediately.

Since then, Upper North has become the most expensive neighborhood in the city with a median home value of $500,000.[7] It is currently populated by 70,000 fairly segregated people: young professionals living in luxury condos, wealthy (predominantly White) families in renovated three-story row houses, and work-ing-class (predominantly Black and Latino) families in rent-controlled housing. In a city with a 20% poverty rate and 63% percent people of color, only 8% of the neighborhood's population is below the poverty line and just 25% are people of color. While the median income of the city is close to $45,000 per year, the median of Upper North is $140,000 with more than 80% of its residents holding bachelors degrees or higher. It is part of a solidly liberal voting district that has supported the rise of several prominent Democratic politicians.

Though its public schools enjoy national rankings in academics and athletics, there are many prestigious private schools in Upper North that primarily recruit from local families. In fact, two-thirds of families in the neighborhood (mostly White) send their children to private schools. One of the oldest and most prestig-ious of these is Kent Academy, which sits a few blocks from a popular park along one of the main streets in the neighborhood. Large gates cordon off the property, but are swung open by traffic police who direct parents' cars at the beginning of each day. The original building has long since been concealed by several renova-tions; the overall effect is a modern blend of brick and glass. A stairway leads to the main doors, which spill into a hotel-like lobby. A front desk houses a security guard who politely asked me to sign in most days but otherwise required no form of identification.

As might be expected of a school that charges steep tuition (upwards of $30,000 a year), the facilities are truly impressive: a state-of-the-art auditorium, gym, labs, and library as well as classrooms fully loaded with audiovisual equip-ment. The school's several floors are built around a beautiful courtyard; its carpeted hallways, flooded with natural light and filled with potted plants, provide spaces for students to study, eat, and rest, giving the feel of a home or cozy dormi-tory. In contrast with the institutionalized herding responding to a bell at the end of each class period at West High, Kent has student-selected music playing between classes as kids saunter through the halls in groups of two or three. Though there is surely a social hierarchy here (it is, after all, a high school), it is not so obvious as it was at West. At Kent, the students all seem of a piece: almost every girl I saw has long, straight hair and wears a similar combination of boots and tights under a casual dress. Most of the boys have a look of cultivated dishevelment with bed-head hair and slouchy pants and shirts. Almost all of the students I see are White. A few of the faculty and most of the support staff are not.

Kent's mission hangs in poster form at the end of each hallway and was referenced by every (yes, *every*) person I met. In general, the mission states that students should be educated within a school environment that is humane and joyful where respect and trust help nurture a disposition towards self-discipline, reflection, and action rooted in integrity, confidence, and empathy. It mentions imagination, curiosity, the cultivation of diverse perspectives, and collaboration between students and teachers. It is a rather long statement that is rooted in the principles of progressive educators and a multicultural democracy. In tension with this lofty rhetoric, however, is the truth that this is still a private school that boasts competitive admissions processes and a steep tuition. Intriguingly, several teachers told me that many parents send their children to the school with little or no regard for the mission despite its uniqueness; they simply want their children to attend a prestigious school and Kent is one of the most elite in the city.

The Students

After a brief introduction to my research in Liz Johnson's two sections of a required American history course for juniors, twelve students agreed to participate. All but one was White and all but two self-identified as being from upper-class families. Melanie, the daughter of working-class Chinese immigrants attended Kent on scholarship, and Cora, a White girl whose father was a public school teacher and mother was a graphic designer attended Kent thanks to an inheritance from her grandmother. The rest of the students were legacies of alumni, lived nearby, and, subsequently, knew each other well even if they did not socialize together outside of school. They all identified as coming from wealthy families: Dylan's father owned a large chain of grocery stores, Paige's grandfather had been a wealthy entrepreneur (described by history books as a "robber baron"), and Dallas' mother was an acclaimed author. The others' parents (mostly fathers) were primarily powerful lawyers or worked in finance (see Table 3.2).

Exceptional Students: "That Makes Us Different"

As an outside observer, it is easy to categorize both West Town and Upper North as "bubbles" in that they are demographically homogeneous communities of primarily White, relatively affluent people whose lives are literally bound by geographic isolation from people different than them in terms of race and class. What is perplexing, however, is that only the participants from West Town described their community in this way, and did so overwhelmingly. Kent students, rather, seemed to be almost purposefully talking around the term by calling their neighborhood a "cluster" or "sphere" that was "safe" and "clean" compared with the rest of the city; their school was a "homey" and "comfortable" "haven" or "utopia." Dylan portrayed the neighborhood as an "enclave of privileged kids":

> Basically everybody who lives in Upper North—we live a very, you know, a life of a lot of resources and the houses are nice. Like, the streets are nice. There's nice shopping area and everything.

TABLE 3.2 Liz Johnson's Students

Student	Race	Economic status	Years at the school	Political affiliation
Adam	White	Upper Class	Elementary, Middle, High	Undecided
Cora	White	Middle Class	High	Liberal
Dallas	White	Upper Class	Elementary, Middle, High	Independent/ Liberal
Dylan	White	Upper Class	Elementary, Middle, High	Liberal
Elliott	White	Upper Class	Elementary, Middle, High	Undecided
Hattie	White	Upper Class	Elementary, Middle, High	Liberal
Jane	White	Upper Class	Elementary, Middle, High	Undecided
Jennifer	White	Upper Class	High	Conservative
Max	White	Upper Class	Elementary, Middle, High	Independent/Conservative
Melanie	Asian-American	Working Class	High	Undecided
Paige	White	Upper Class	Elementary, Middle, High	Undecided
Rachel	White	Upper Class	Elementary, Middle, High	Undecided

In her description of the typical Upper North resident, Rachel expressed a connection between "good" and "bad" elements embedded with her notions of race and class:

> They're probably a middle to upper class White person, but then there's also worse parts of every area.

Many voluntarily compared themselves to other kids noting how much more worldly they were in comparison to their suburban counterparts. According to Jennifer:

> It's hard to be bored here because there's so much going on, and you're exposed to a lot more than—like, we almost moved to the suburbs and I know a lot of people in the suburbs, and I feel like you're exposed to a lot more in the city. The suburbs are very sheltered. Almost everyone's the same, which is very unfortunate.

Though their school was less diverse racially and socio-economically than West, the Kent students consistently described themselves as "open" to the "real world" in ways the suburban kids were not simply by nature of their living within the city limits.

This was true even when comparing themselves with kids who attended other schools in Upper North. For example, Roberts Academy, a similarly elite rival private school drawing from the same general pool of families, had no commitments to progressive education or social justice. Kent kids frequently compared themselves favorably to Roberts' students in terms of both academics and behavior. Jennifer, who had attended both schools, compared them this way:

> Roberts is really academically competitive and so the people are mean and it doesn't have any sense of community and the administration controls everything. ... At Kent, you can do a lot more things that you enjoy without being judged for it. And academics are just as tough, like, people are like, "Oh my God, Roberts is so much harder because we have APs." But honestly, Kent's classes don't need to be branded with "AP" to be tough.

Rachel agreed that Kent's progressive curriculum was better than Roberts because it produced people who cared more about the world:

> At Kent we're not only taught the basics, like U.S. history, math, and science, but we're also taught to care about like the bigger issues, such as the drug war or homelessness or whatever else we learn about. And we're also taught that you don't have to be a mathematician or a banker to succeed, but you can do something bigger.

Paige noted that this emphasis on being good people positioned them as less academically rigorous than Roberts students, a thesis she challenged:

> I am really nervous to say I go to Kent because a lot of city kids have a negative view of it as where stupid rich kids go to school. And I completely disagree with that statement because I think that while our curriculum is incredibly academic, we're also just like smart, street-smart, kids in general I think.

She went on the describe the Kent students as

> Less flashy than a lot of other schools would think we were. We're a lot more down to earth, and the Roberts girls always have their nails done, their hair always looks nice. Maybe that's just the ones I've been seeing. I mean, obviously, there's a few, but the general population I wouldn't feel is that way here. So I think that Kent is a lot better than Roberts.

In one of only two mentions of a "bubble" by a Kent student, Jennifer explained how she grapples with being "privileged" in relation to students at Roberts:

> I mean, I personally don't like to think of myself as privileged because that makes me sound pretentious and the truth of the matter is that I *am*, and I know that that sounds awful to say because people don't like to think of

themselves that way. That would not be a negative thing to say at Roberts. Like Hunter Colby flaunts the fact that she lives in this mansion and she had like an internship with a huge designer. But at Kent you don't like to think of yourself as privileged because you like to just, I mean, I think we have more of an awareness of what goes on outside our little Kent bubble. Like I don't like to think of myself as privileged but I know that I am. I think it's definitely downplayed more here than it as at Roberts.

Rachel also mentioned a bubble when she framed Kent as the "right" kind of private school:

I think when you're with people that are like you, like at Kent you don't feel uncomfortable about your affluence or anything. And when you're with people that are less fortunate, you feel maybe you don't want to go out and say all the things that you can do and where you are going for summer vacation. It might be more comfortable to have them segregated, but then at the same time the people segregated in the lower class are not given the opportunity to see what's out there to see what they could be if they, like, become successful and got a good education and moved out of their neighborhood. I think at the right segregated upper-class school, we know what that lower class is missing out on and what we could help them gain if we like worked with them or something, whereas if you're at the wrong segregated upper-class school like Roberts, you just are in your bubble and you don't know what's happening.

According to Jane,

At least people are conscious of issues at Kent. Whether or not we do anything, at least we know what we are *supposed* to do.

While they were proud of and grateful for their school's progressive mission, a few students dug deeper to reflect on the mismatch between its rhetoric and its lack of racial and economic diversity. Their criticism had gathered steam in the months before my visit because of several letters to the editor in the school paper demanding to know why there were not more students of color at the school.[8] Dallas positioned this tension as inevitable given the school's status:

There's this unavoidable irony that we put so much emphasis on diversity and social justice, but there's just, like, the fact that we pay the tuition that we do to go to this school. You know, it just makes it so that there's a certain demographic of kids here.

One of the most provocative and revealing quotes came from Cora, who described the school this way:

> It's sort of like we don't really want to be what we are, so that makes us different because we're not willing to sit there and let it become like an all-White, all-rich school—but, like, we sort of are.

Overall, the students were well versed in the tenets of progressive education and saw their schooling as a key factor distinguishing them in positive ways from other privileged students in that they were more aware and more concerned about the rest of the world.

When discussing times they left Upper North or interacted with people from other parts of the city, many of the students reflected on how they would actively downplay their background for fear of being stereotyped in ways they did not want to be or having their lifestyle criticized without someone first getting to know them. When talking about the times she left the neighborhood to perform music, for example, Dylan admitted to feeling "sheltered" and expressed a desire to get to know people before they found out where she was from to avoid negative stereotypes.

> We met these people there and they were like, "Oh we could hang out sometime." And I was thinking, "Where do we hang out?" Because I don't want people over at my house because I feel bad. It's just something, like, I've always tried to like hide, like, where I'm from when I go to new places because, and it's interesting because I feel like everything I've been granted going to this school, like living in the way that I do, has been a dream. You know, I feel ashamed of it sometimes. … Whenever I meet people from some other sphere that isn't Kent or Upper North or this affluent grouping, I always feel kind of really embarrassed at first. It's just that they assume that you don't care about people besides yourself, and you are centered in a very materialistic environment and that you—it's just friction that, you know, there's a kind of a mutual understanding between you and the other person that you have been given certain things that other people haven't. And, like, do you deserve it? Like, do *I* deserve it? And when someone doesn't know you that well—once I'm friends with someone, like, they can come over to my house because they know me, but, like, the generalizations that could be made that I'm undeserving, that I get anything that I want, don't have to work for any-thing—I just don't think it equates with who I am. I just think they would think of me in like a pre-judged way, like I'm the rich girl, the girl who goes to private school, the girl who lives in Upper North in this house.

Paige similarly recollected:

> I had to do this assignment where we had to go to this public magnet school and we had to interview kids and we made sure to dress really

simple, like, we didn't want to look like we stood out or anything like that. Then we'd go up to kids and said we were from Kent and they said, "Ooh." They were just really uncomfortable. We made an effort. We went back to my house and changed, got in a cab, and made sure we didn't have nice things hanging off of us, because you don't want somebody to judge you based on what you look like. So I think that's one of the things that other kids think when they think of Kent—just like rich, White kids.

Though they did so with caution, Kent students seemed to position themselves as above the world in that their awareness of and desire for a better society somehow distinguished them from others within the current dysfunctional reality. Max told me that,

I think we kind of believe that we're sort of invincible because to an extent we are. There's not a whole lot that sticks to us.

Kent students had an awareness and deep understanding of social issues as well as a confidence interacting in the world that their peers had not yet developed. With this confidence, however, came a concern that others would judge them unfavorably; they were quick to distance themselves from such people and to distinguish themselves as thoughtful, aware, and down-to-earth kids. They were, in a word, exceptional. Dallas even joked that they were the "chosen people."

Overall, the Kent students characterized their lifestyle in Upper North the following ways: 1) it has the benefits of the suburbs (primarily safety, "good schools," and cleanliness) without sheltering its residents; 2) it is something to downplay when interacting with people from other places; and 3) though exclusive, their progressive schooling provides them an opportunity to distinguish themselves from other elite students in the neighborhood.

At Ease

The recent ethnographic work of Shamus Khan (2011) building on Bourdieuan notions of class distinction, reproduction of cultural capital, and habitus is quite useful here. In his research with students at an elite boarding school, he found them rejecting a sense of entitlement in order to embody an ease of being in the world. Rather than the classic privileged ethic of exclusion and distinction through elite taste-making, the upper-class students in his study embraced an ethic of inclusion and a radical egalitarianism in terms of their cultural preferences (e.g., valuing diversity, balancing "high" and "popular" culture, wanting to appear down-to-earth).

For students at Kent, there was a great emphasis on distinguishing themselves from their privileged peers by downplaying a classical sense of distinction. The uniqueness they were quick and proud to discuss was their progressive education that made them aware of the world and their sense of commitment that they had a responsibility to engage it. This presents an interesting tension, and was one that Khan found in his work at St. Paul's. In contrast with previous elite attitudes obsessed with pedigree, this new outlook is connected to an understanding of the world as naturally hierarchical based upon experiences rather than birthright; in other words, it is not who you are but what you have done that rightfully positions you at the top. When hierarchies are so naturalized, the connection between birth and experience is obfuscated. And when ease is privileged above entitlement, those who do not fit in tend to be those from marginalized backgrounds without the means to live in such a worldly fashion.

Most notably, I found the embrace of an embodied ease in the world to be endemic at Kent and almost non-existent at West High. For example, the West kids were shier in terms of stating their opinions in class than were the Kent students. If West students spoke in front of the class, they were almost always asking a question, presenting factual information for a project, or answering a question of Vernon's. The Kent students who spoke up, on the other hand, more often did so to express their opinion and articulate their position on an issue being discussed, implying an understanding of themselves as people whose opinions mattered and should be heard. Though certainly interested in the topics and outspoken in our interviews, the West students seemed much more timid or uncomfortable expressing opinions about similar issues in front of their class. Conversely, none of the outspoken Kent kids expressed any sentiment that they were sheltered or too young to position themselves in relation to a controversial topic.

Another way that these schools differed with regards to embodying ease in the world compared with segregating themselves in a bubble is evidenced by something as taken for granted as a school's front-desk policies. In the suburban bubble, residents are extremely aware of the "dangerous outside" and take action to govern any visitors attempting to enter. Though she knew me well given my daily visits, the security guard at the front door of West High scanned my license every day to issue a photo ID that signified my official permission to be inside the bubble. This consistent vigilance was impressive, especially given the fact that violent crime in West Town is almost non-existent.

While Upper North reports more crime (much less than the rest of the city, of course, but higher than West Town) and carries significantly higher numbers of unknown people commuting through it than does the suburban campus, I simply waved hello to the front desk guard as I walked upstairs each day. Certainly, my appearance and carriage implied an ease and confidence which no doubt facilitated my unmolested entrance, yet the porous nature of the school and the encouragement to move within and beyond its borders were clear. The "open campus" rules at both schools follow these trends: only West High's juniors and seniors had permission to leave campus for lunch and still needed official passes if they were ever in the halls outside of a passing period. Kent students, on the other hand, were free to come and go both inside and outside of the school at any time; their personal responsibility to handle such freedom and comfort were clearly an expectation of the community and evidence of ease in the world rather than an attempt to protect them within a sheltered bubble.

Disturbing the Comfortable

Instead of bursting a metaphorical bubble with the self-described sheltered students, a social justice pedagogy for Kent students often included finding ways to make them uneasy and to challenge the perception that they are above issues of injustice, however aware of them they may be in an abstract or analytical way. When describing her teaching, Liz Johnson thus emphasized the importance of comforting the disturbed and disturbing the comfortable.

> You can't just target the oppressed. I mean, I don't think my kids are the oppressors, but they belong to the oppressor class more or less, so I don't know if I'm characterizing that in a way I'm totally comfortable with, but the cages need to be rattled and that's what I'm doing. And the challenge is to try to do that in a way that doesn't freak people out and doesn't impose a political agenda. I mean it *is* a political agenda, although it's not me indoctrinating my views. It's more exposing them to a structure of values that is humanist as opposed to selfish. … I have this motto: comfort the disturbed and disturb the comfortable.

When describing her teaching, Liz emphasized the need to expose students to sophisticated issues that were living and current. The lessons she organized and readings she assigned clearly fit the idea of talking about "real" issues and "disturbing" students' assumptions about the world. For example, in referencing class and racial issues in class, she reminded them of the Founding Fathers' "conservative power grab":

> There's a line I draw down the middle of the class pyramid—essentially, the Patriot elites convinced the lower class through the Declaration of Independence, which is propaganda sewing up the bonds of social Whiteness with the political and economic powers concentrated at the top, that they share social power through Whiteness and they share political power a bit. To this day, they don't share the economic power. But now you've got a nation built around ideals that people buy into because they think it creates equality but it doesn't and it was never intended to.

Students were quite familiar with this diagram; none seemed shocked by such an interpretation of American history and seemed to take it for granted as a "normal" way to understand modern society.

Unlike Vernon, Liz's aim was not to "cross over" any line or "expose" students to the real world given that her students already considered themselves immersed in it from a hierarchical position. Because they embodied the "ease" that Khan (2011) describes in his depiction of the new elite, it makes sense that Liz hoped to trouble their comfort by positioning privileged people within a critical theoretical perspective of American history, highlighting ways disturbed people had and could be comforted, and, ultimately, disturbing the interpretative frameworks students used to maintain their comfortable position.

Whereas the challenge for Vernon was in avoiding the reification of an Us/Them binary by embracing the metaphor of a bubble, Liz faced the risk of reifying students' ease in seeking to disturb it. By engaging students in questions that troubled their worldviews and confronting them with the facts and figures of injustice, she was certainly "disturbing" their intellects (and, importantly, their hearts). However, it was remarkably easy for students to incorporate this disturbance into a heightened feeling of exceptionalism (So few other privileged students think about the world the way we do! So few other people get it!). The seductive element of this exceptionalism is that, in one way, it is true. Very few other elite schools have as a mission the disturbance of their students' conceptions of privilege and justice in any way. The dangerous element, however, is that any disturbance with the potential to rupture hegemonic forms is neutralized as students incorporate it into their sense of ease. In her best moments, Liz patiently guarded students' discomfort as pedagogically important and prevented them from so easily escaping back into their comfortable states.

Conclusion

Privilege, it turns out, does not look the same everywhere and we are wise to understand its differences, particularly in terms of how its residents position themselves and how such thinking shapes teachers' pedagogic choices. Though both groups can (and should) be considered "net beneficiary" communities of privilege, this chapter helps to make sense of how the conceptualizations of community among students in one elite private urban school serving primarily upper-class students differed in important, nuanced ways from those views of students in a public suburban school serving primarily upper-middle-class students. A model of teaching such as social justice pedagogy, with its potentially controversial, sophisticated analytics and unpredictable interactions with the real world, must not be applied (or analyzed) without considering such factors as the restrictions created by the courses themselves within particular school cultures and the dynamics influenced by students' social class and cultures. I now turn to examining this pedagogy in action, with special attention to how these different conceptions of their community and selves shaped two different philosophies: *bursting the bubble* and *disturbing the comfortable*.

4

SOCIAL JUSTICE PEDAGOGY IN ACTION

"Bursting the Bubble" and "Disturbing the Comfortable"

> Interrupting the cultural production of privilege requires intentional efforts on the part of educators to confront and transform lessons students learn about their place in the world and their relations with others. By creating instructional settings—in and outside of the classroom context—that interrupt privilege, we can be more certain about what lessons we are actually teaching students about themselves and others.
>
> *(Howard, 2008, p. 228)*

Keeping in mind how students positioned themselves as being sheltered from or exceptional within the world, I now turn my attention to exploring the distinctive philosophies and pedagogies of two social justice teachers in communities of privilege: Vernon Sloan, a public school teacher at a secondary school in an affluent suburb, and Liz Johnson, a private school teacher at an elite downtown academy. Though similar in many regards, there are significant differences in how Vernon and Liz approached social justice pedagogy in their classrooms. These differences can be attributed primarily to their personal histories, their school contexts, and the social-class positions of their students, and manifest themselves in two distinctive philosophies: *bursting the bubble* and *disturbing the comfortable*.

These distinctive approaches remind us that good teaching need not look the same; in fact, it should be thoughtfully adapted to the context in which it is enacted. In the suburbs, Vernon's philosophy of "bursting the bubble" emphasized identifying socioeconomic boundaries and encouraging students to cross them. The primary challenge within this framework lay in addressing issues of injustice without exoticizing the Other, romanticizing the plight of marginalized people, or reifying deficit stereotypes about people from different racial, ethnic, and social-class groups. Liz, on the other hand, sought to "disturb the comfortable" and "comfort the disturbed" of her urban students. By engaging students in questions that troubled their worldviews and confronting them with the facts and figures of injustice, she was certainly "disturbing" their intellects (and, importantly, their hearts). However, it was remarkably easy for students to translate this disturbance into a heightened feeling of exceptionalism and to incorporate ruptures to their ways of thinking into their original sense of ease. How did they justify teaching for social justice with privileged students? What did they see as their ultimate goals? How did they balance teaching about individual perpetuations of injustice with attention to structural causes of oppression? And, perhaps most importantly, how did this impact their curriculum and instruction?

To answer these questions, this chapter is divided into two case studies. For each case, I first describe the teachers' personalities and backgrounds in order to make sense of how their histories and politics influenced their teaching. I then describe their philosophies-in-action in terms of course content, classroom practices, and community connections. The case studies are followed by a comparative analysis examining the strategies these teachers used to negotiate the tensions and challenges inherent in social justice pedagogy within privileged communities: how to balance attention to justice with preparation for post-secondary elite education, how to balance a strong social critique with a respect for multiple perspectives, and how to do this kind of teaching in the face of logistical constraints. These tensions have no easy resolution; those who attempt to untangle them deserve commendation and encouragement as well as critique. Documenting the pedagogic choices and strategies of these teachers not only expands our ability to determine what is possible and desirable within these classrooms, but is also an important step in determining how and why their students responded in a variety of ways, the focus of Chapter 5.

Case One: Social Justice Pedagogy in the Suburbs

Vernon Sloan

Amidst such a homogeneous and clean-scrubbed environs as West Town and its high school, Vernon Sloan's classroom stood out. On my first visit to the school, I asked a student for directions to his room. The student laughed at the idea that someone may confuse it with any other spot and said, "Mr. Sloan's? It's crazy— you can't miss it. Just follow the bumper stickers." Sure enough, I could see his room from the opposite end of the hallway. Political posters of every persuasion spilled out from the door like dangling bits of clothes from an over-stuffed suitcase. Inside, it was a challenge to find any inch of wall or ceiling not covered by flags, posters, stickers, photographs, or life-size cardboard cutouts of famous political figures.[1] Fifteen bookshelves brimmed with books labeled by topic: Feminist Theory, Satire & Humor, Black Nationalism, etc. Thirty desks sat together in two concentric U-shapes to face the front of the room where there was a white board, a podium, and a chair for Vernon. Pictures of his family and his bike, always propped up at the front of the room ready for the commute home, hinted at a rich life beyond the school.

A thirty-year teaching veteran, Vernon stood out at West Town High as much as his classroom did. He had long hair that touched his shoulders (though he later cut it short because he was "tired of being called a hippie by people who don't know what that means") and wore Teva-like sandals that offset the White middle-class suburban dad uniform of khaki pants and a tucked-in shirt. In speech, dress, and interactions with the students, Vernon concertedly cultivated a contradictory identity intended to challenge their assumptions about him.

> I don't even like the word "hippie." I just don't like stereotypes. I think that is why I spend so much time in the weight room, totally to counteract the stereotype. That whole thing of being an athlete and being "man enough"— that's bad.

When in the hallways or in front of class, he wore a bemused look on his face and chatted with kids as they walked by his door. Quick to laugh or crack a joke, he seemed to put students in a good mood and often gave high fives and hugs. He could be known to "lay down the law" with a kid, however, and steer a conversation into intellectual or political territory at a moment's notice; this ability seemed to intimidate the students and created an aura of sorts around Vernon. When describing him, many students mentioned his deep intelligence, his Leftist politics, and his rare talent of treating them like "real people" instead of "just kids." A few described him as a "legendary" and a refreshingly "different" teacher at the school.

Vernon is a fifth-generation teacher, the grandson of a professor who had been called to testify before the House of Un-American Activities Committee because of his involvement with the peace and labor movements and the son of a social activist who hobnobbed with leading figures in the civil-rights movement. These radical roots extend beyond politics into religion, as preachers are common in his family tree. These spiritual and secular influences have greatly shaped his progressive politics and activism in the anti-nuclear movement, as well as political campaigns for candidates like Jesse Jackson. Said Vernon:

> I am motivated by that ethic—that Christian ethic, that democratic ethic that, you know, we are here to care for each other.

In fact, he told me (tongue only partially in cheek) that he justified his job in a suburban school as a way for him to be a "suburban missionary" to "save the lost souls of affluent youth." His spiritual and political background also influenced his and his wife's decision to raise their three young children in the Quaker tradition and to home school them.

Despite building a life in the suburbs over the past ten years, Vernon expressed great angst about whether this has been a good choice.

> My wife wants to commit class suicide because she's so sick of the material-ism and the objects we acquire and we see that our kids pretty much expect that, you know? But, on the other hand, some of those values aren't—why would we commit class suicide? Isn't it something that we strive to allow everybody to have—health care, to have an adequate house, giving them access to communication and mass media? But mass *consumption*—that's a whole other world. I guess we would like to live a simpler life within it. I mean, otherwise, that's an ascetic, right, to give up all material things and work for the good? I don't know if I'm capable of that. I don't know if I'm willing to ask that of students, either. Maybe I'm fooling myself because I think that there's enough for everybody.

He is quite clear about how rampant "affluenza" is in West Town and works hard to avoid being sucked into "the middle-class myth/illusion" that is strong in the suburbs. "Much of my life has been spent either consumed with the mirage or fight-ing the influence it has had on me," he notes. Like his students, he describes the suburbs as a "bubble" and makes a conscious effort to "burst" it as much as possible.

Born and raised in the city, Vernon left his beloved hometown to study education at a small liberal arts school but moved back to marry his college sweetheart. There was never any doubt he would become a teacher. After working for a few years at a Catholic boys' school in the city, he got a job at West Town High in the early 1980s to which he commuted from a neighborhood famous for its progressive politics and racial diversity where he and his first wife wanted to raise their daughter. Once he remarried and moved to the suburbs, he made sense of his work this way:

> There is this idea that you need to work and live in a community and all interconnect, to witness. I feel like my role here is just as important [as working in the city]. My father's good friend [a nationally prominent Black civil-rights activist] said you can't go into the city and talk about this stuff— you have to go back to *your* community to teach it.

Their choice of residence is one he and his wife frequently debate, however; the idea of moving back to the city seems to attract them both and is a distinct possibility after Vernon retires in a few years when there is no longer a need to commute to West.

Urban History at West Town High School

The course Vernon recommended I study was "Urban History," a weighted social studies elective investigating the history of the city—his favorite class to teach.

According to Vernon, the teacher who originated the course wanted it to be weighted to "weed out the bad kids." Though he disagreed with that sentiment, Vernon and his colleague Tom (who taught three other sections of the class) continued to advocate the weighting of the course because it allowed it status as a "special topics" class, which meant it was exempt from many of the school board's more stringent general curriculum approval rules. Whereas the original teacher had only taught one section and sought to keep it that way, Vernon's influence on the course and his recruitment of students had increased it to seven sections.

Content

The introduction of the syllabus reminded students of the course's more traditional academic requirements:

> This is a weighed class and therefore you will be expected to give a weighted effort. There will be copious amounts of reading assigned, profuse amounts of essential questions to be discussed, abundant enduring understandings to be discovered and plentiful opportunities for you to demonstrate your mastery of the history of the city.

Vernon told me those students who could not keep with the reading, whether for academic or language challenges, were encouraged to drop the course. Two-week units included an "Introduction to Urban History," "Capital and Labor History," "Neighborhood Apartheid or Ethnic Purity?," "Architecture Amongst Human-made and Natural Disasters," "Gangs and the Underground Economy," and "The Political Tradition," complemented by shorter three-day units at the end of the semester: "Pedagogical, Literary and Intellectual Heritage," "Music and the City," "The Athletic Tradition," and "The End of the Suburbs?" On the first day, Vernon issued two required texts to his students (books written by professional historians about the history of the city) and an inch-thick course reader filled with copied articles. Students were tested on their assigned reading with weekly quizzes and multiple-choice tests. The remainder of their grade was made up of classroom participation and project presentations. Extra credit was available through volunteering at different agencies in the city and attending approved events related to the city's history and culture.

Though he felt pressured by Tom to include "mainstream" history of the city (most notably a dry, non-critical unit filled with accounts of mayoral terms), Vernon worked hard to incorporate current and historical issues of the city involving race and social class. He frequently assigned readings and showed documentary clips about the Black middle class, violence against laborers, middle-class reformers, the de-ethnicization of White people, gentrification, and racial segregation. Additionally, Vernon frequently referenced critical scholars like historian Howard Zinn, educator Bill Ayers, and feminist Mary Daly. The bookshelves in his classroom brimmed with books by similarly radical authors that beckoned to students (a few of whom even requested them as loans).

Rarely a day went by when some injustice of the past was not briefly connected to some issue in the local present; housing policy in West Town, the difficulties of African American students moving to West Town from the city, racial profiling at the school, the way immigrant day laborers are treated by their parents, etc. For example, Vernon told them, "I get incensed when I think about Mexican laborers here in West Town. Does anyone remember the immigration demonstration and what the paper's headline was about that?" One kid does: "The Day the Grass Grew." Instead of focusing on the immigrants, Vernon explained, the paper focused on the "poor businessmen who had to struggle without their workers." "They would actually publish that?" asked Mel, incredulously. "Do you remember that?" Vernon inquired. "I talked about it with some people," offered Fred.

Throughout the semester, Vernon explicitly called out racism, homophobia, class struggle, and patriarchy that exist in West Town. "All of these are social constructs," he explained to the kids early on in the semester, "but they're real. Because I'm heterosexual, I can talk about my family and my kids. If I were gay, could I speak freely and openly about being gay?" Several students scoffed out loud, indicating that he could not. "In West Town we have gay couples. Did you hear about the second-grade birthday boycott?" He then went on to explain how several parents had refused to send their children to a birthday party because gay parents were hosting it. On another day, Vernon showed the students maps of racial and social class demographics in relation to housing patterns and told them that

> The rich moved out and built highways like a toilet where they would send their crap while building their 'beautiful' burbs. It benefits us to the deficit of those who live there. It's a pearl necklace. I'm not saying it's our fault, but it's our responsibility. Toilets leave shit behind. The environment has been degraded—literally. If you read Jonathan Kozol—the hospital incinerators are always in the worst neighborhoods.

For most of the students, this was the first time an adult had openly discussed the connection between urban decay and suburban comfort so frankly.

Students' in-class responses to this context was mixed. They considered the readings he assigned to be "hoop homework" and, once they realized they could earn a high grade in the course without completing it every night, the majority of them stopped doing it. During most of the in-class documentary clips, students' interest level seemed low as many of them would chat with each other softly, lay their heads on their backpacks, text under their desks, or doodle. Vernon would shout questions over the narrator or pause the film to make a point, though these pedagogic interruptions rarely led to any sustained discussion. This seemed to be a loss for the students as many of his questions were truly provocative. For instance, during a film about the abuse of factory workers in the early 20th century and the reformers who tried to support them, Vernon called out about one famous woman, "Was she reasonable or was she radical?" No one responded and he un-paused the film.

The few assignments students had were often shared in presentations to the class with the intention they would "teach each other" about a particular aspect of a time period or issue. These were rather tedious affairs; it seemed as if Vernon and I were the only ones who regularly listened. Other students would sit staring ahead with glazed eyes or heads slumped on backpacks atop their desks. Vernon addressed this "monotony" with the class by developing quizzes with questions from each presentation and by asking for student feedback to improve the projects. Similarly perfunctory was the online component of the class. Every few weeks, Vernon would post a question in a discussion forum to which students were required to post an answer. Most students posted a comment to complete the requirement or neglected to post anything; there were very few interactive exchanges. The one student who admitted to reading someone else's posts only did so because she had a crush on the boy who wrote them.

It's important to note that the students expressed a deep appreciation for this strategy and found Vernon's class to be a site of genuine curiosity rather than feigned interest for a grade. Brian explained why Vernon's class was so valuable to him:

> People like Mr. Sloan make West Town not as much a bubble, except for a few things. Sloan is not the same as everyone else, and, like, the bubble—it doesn't disappear, but it changes and contorts to different things because of him.

They agreed with him that homework typically distracted from what they called "real learning" and prevented them from being more naturally engaged. John told me:

> We loved it when Sloan would just sit up there and talk because you can learn so much from his stories. I would rather do that than a worksheet. I am not going to remember a worksheet; I mean, come on.

One assignment that did spark significant creativity was the final project for which students interviewed people native to the city to ask them about their experiences related to race and social class. The students video-recorded their conversations and played the most provocative segments for the class. The interviews with family members and acquaintances provided a wealth of stories that were shocking, sad, moving, and revelatory. Many students said the assignment felt "crammed in" at the end of the semester, and expressed a desire to have had more time to share their interviews with their peers and to hear the interviews of others.

Classroom Practices

Few of Vernon's class periods involved traditional planned activities with formalized objectives. Rather, a typical day in Urban History began with Vernon standing or sitting at the front of the classroom in the center of the double-row U-shaped desk arrangement asking provocative rhetorical questions about current events or relaying his own philosophical musings and stories. These often seemed initially tangential but would eventually connect to the official topics of the day. His personal beliefs, influences, and experiences in these ramblings were always on full display, something the students universally told me in interviews that they enjoyed and appreciated.

Embedded within his commentary was a caustic humor that seemed to diffuse tension around particularly taboo topics like race. One mid-winter day as kids were sauntering in for class, he teased a White girl about her tan to which she responded that she "didn't fake bake." "How did you get your tan, Henry?" he asked the only Black student in class. Henry laughed and said, "Yeah, I'm just *really* tan." Another time, he was telling the students about the importance of dialects in the city and asked a former student who popped her head into the room to say hello if she knew how to "speak White." The girl, a Black transplant from the city new to West Town in the last year, laughed and said, "Hey, I have to speak White all the time." He often teased kids about falling prey to stereotypes of suburban life, referring to them as "privileged people" on a regular basis, and bantering with them about being "sheltered WASPs." Importantly, Vernon implicated himself in the jokes and made note of "how limited our knowledge is as suburbanites" when learning about the issues of and people in the city.

During these monologues, it was not unusual for Vernon to identify a stereotype of life in the suburbs and "flip" it for the students to interrogate from another perspective. At the beginning of class one day early in the semester, he told the kids about how much he misses living in the city: "Now that I live here with all the White people, I lock my doors—all the corporate criminals and the people who start wars." He waited for a reaction, then said, "I'm kidding, but I'm not," which became a common refrain. Another afternoon he asked students to tell him which parts of the city were "dangerous." A few kids mentioned public housing populated primarily by Black families that was famous for drugs, crime, and poverty. "Ahh," responded Vernon. "But if you're Black, you would never go to Braxton [a predominantly blue-collar White neighborhood]. Two Black kids were beaten unconscious there a few years back. Why is it that if we go through a certain neighborhood, there will be video surveillance but not at the stock market which is where you can get the really good drugs?" Questions like this were more often than not rhetorical devices that only touched upon complex topics demanding more attention, but provoked students nonetheless.

Though all were intrigued by these kinds of comments, some students admitted to feeling confused about whether Vernon was trying to challenge their stereotypes of the city or expose them to a life that was very different than their own so they would appreciate their community more. "Look," Vernon said one day, "the race issue is very clearly an issue in the city. Living in West Town is a privilege. We have huge backyards, fancy parks—where I used to teach downtown, we would have to clean the soccer field every day before practice to make sure there wasn't any broken glass in the field." He compared that with a little-used, new $300,000 park in West Town where his young kids play. Later in the semester, a girl admitted to being scared about going into the city to research an "ethnic neighborhood." "Gangbangers won't kill a White girl," Vernon told her with a smile. He nods my way and says, "I know that Katy knows why I say things, but I want you all to understand that sometimes I say things flippantly— I just want you to know. I don't want to make you afraid, I just want you to be conscious." "Yeah—the buildings are made of knives," cracked Mel (to which the class laughed in response). In an interview after class, Mel confessed that,

> Like, sometimes I don't know what he wants. Like, he'll say, "They're people. They're real people." I know that. But then he'll say like, "Gangs. Seriously. They totally exist. When you go into the city, don't get fucked up." I don't know what he really wants—maybe he doesn't know.

Calling out students' privilege, then, was sometimes accompanied with a critique of the systemic inequities from which it stems and, other times, with emphasis on not taking for granted what they had relative to others. Though not always mutually exclusive, these messages could conflict and some students struggled to make sense of them. At the end of the semester, Vernon wrote this quote on the board: "The problem with stereotypes is not that they are untrue, but that they are incomplete." It seemed to be his attempt to present an idea that would challenge their mainstream images of urban and suburban life while acknowledging the real differences between them, but may have been too little, too late to deeply engage the students.

Despite his centrality as a classroom figure whose personal stories drove class conversation, Vernon maintained that the "best learning" happened when he spoke "as little as possible." A few of the more outspoken students would interrupt his stories, leading to repartee for which the other students were engaged spectators. Slowly but surely, students' questions and comments became more frequent and more critical as the semester progressed. In the last month, it was not unusual for students to ask questions like Claire's in response to learning about a natural disaster in the city's history: "Was it a certain group that was affected or was it everyone?" Students who had never talked about race before were now naming it with more comfort. One particularly vibrant exchange occurred when discussing reform legislation of the Progressive Era. The following vignette comes from my field notes.

> Vernon asks, "When they talk about housing, are there neighborhoods Black people wouldn't want to move into?" "Obviously south of Front Street with the Irish neighborhoods," says one kid. Xavier adds, "My dad used to live in Jefferson which was mostly White, but there are still homeless people here and there." Vernon asks, "How many White folks live in housing projects? It's predominantly poor and Black. On our field trip to the city, why was José talking about gentrification being a problem? The cheap housing goes away. It's a tricky issue. Like in Maple Bluff there are no for sale signs. It's illegal to do it. Why?" Emma asks, shocked, "It's illegal?" Another student suggests that maybe it's to keep people from knowing who is moving out. Fred says, "It's a chain effect. Property values would decrease." "Exactly," says Vernon. "So people won't know it's empty and there won't be squatters?" suggests Claire. Vernon gives an example of another neighborhood with its many abandoned properties. "We almost moved out there," shares Luna. Vernon starts to say, "In the 1950s, if you were a White, ethnic homeowner in the city—" but is interrupted by many in the class laughing. "What do you mean by 'White ethnic'?" asks Emma. "Polish, Lithuanian, Jewish. And for sale signs go up whenever an African American family moves in. That's exactly what happened in certain neighborhoods in the city. Now we have laws to protect against unscrupulous real-estate agents," Vernon replies. "Why doesn't this go on everywhere?" asks Mel. Vernon's response is typically indirect: "If we're looking back at Victorian times with ethnic strife, an example is the strikes in the city. If companies hire scabs, you're going to draw them in from the South and other countries. You have Blacks do the work Whites won't do and that creates tension between the groups." "But why is Maple Bluff the only neighborhood concerned with racial balance? Is there something offensive in what I asked?" Mel asks. Vernon, again indirectly, says, "There is an Indian and Asian subdivision in West Town behind the woods. Why don't more White folks move up there?" Mel replies: "We almost bought a house up there because obviously I'm Asian and my parents had friends, but the home prices were cheaper someplace else and it was less important for my parents to have a community." "So, it was an economic decision," said Vernon. Mel agrees, "Not about ethnicity." Another student [a White girl] says, "My mom wouldn't buy a house because she saw a lot of African Americans in the neighborhood. People won't move somewhere if they're not comfortable." "We're getting a couple totally different views here," states Vernon. Henry says, "It's how comfortable you feel where you are." Vernon pushes back,

"But that comfort is based on what? Why do people prefer living with similar religious, ethnic identity, socioeconomic status housing? Like, why did I move to this incredibly White island? In Maple Bluff, there was an African American couple across the street, a straight single mom, African American ministers, a lesbian couple, an interracial couple—it was an incredibly diverse block. We gained a progressive reputation because of its policies. West Town has never had policies like that. It gained a reputation of being a conservative suburb." Mel returns to his original question. "Why is Maple Bluff the only one making those policies?" "Well, Maple Bluff is a special place," replies Vernon. "Well, you can't do it citywide, then? Is that the ultimate goal?" pushes Mel. "When we ride through the city, it has bombed out abandoned lots and buildings. The projects are all gone. Where did the underclass go?" Vernon asks. Xavier answers, "The outer suburbs?" Mel laughs and says to Vernon, "You are really good at tip-toeing around questions." "What is a better place to raise kids who are morally sound or physically safe?" Vernon shifts the topic and immediately responds to his own question, "I have a list of ten reasons why the city is better." "Then why aren't you in the city?" asks a student. Mel laughs again, "You are creating more mazes for my questions!" Claire laughs, too, "Are you allergic to answers?" Vernon starts to list his reasons, smiling, "My primary concern for my children is that they see a wider range of gender/sexual expression, much more intense energy. On the other hand, living in the suburbs is good because it's ecologically—my footprint is much less here because I'm not driving to school." A student asks, "Can you live anywhere in the city? Because it's good in some parts, bad in other parts." "But what if your family's income is low? If you lived in the suburbs, it wouldn't be as bad," another says. Xavier counters this statement: "I read an article on how it's a lot harder for financially rocky families to live in the suburbs because there's much less support—it's easier to live in the city where there are food pantries and lower property taxes." Vernon says, "We need those services more and more in the suburbs." Claire says, "I'd live in the suburbs. They're my kids, I want to protect them from crime." Mel says, "All the people will make the decision differently when it's time." Fred says, "In the suburbs, you can take a step back and you're separated from your neighbors. You have more privacy." Vernon challenges him, "But doesn't that lead to isolation? Now I can barely hear my neighbors." "But can't you avoid people you don't know?" Mel asks. Henry says, quietly, "I used to get in fights all the time and then I moved up here, but I shut down completely—I would be a different person. I don't know if it helped me or if it kept me from being who I am." "But that's your choice," Mel fired back. "Well, Mel—" interjects Vernon. "We *all* live in the suburbs," says Mel forcefully as the bell rings, indicating the end of class.

This segment is highly representative of Vernon's meandering style and penchants for tangents, his willingness to name race and social class as important social constructs, and the ways in which his questions generated comments and more questions from students. It is also reflective of the ways that powerful topics got touched upon briefly rather than engaged in depth: Henry's question about whether moving to the suburbs helped him or kept him from being who he really is, Mel's persistent curiosity about why a policy Vernon supports only exists in one small neighborhood in the city, and Xavier's suggestion that there may be better support for low-income families in the city. These are a series of teachable moments that made it to the surface yet seemed to evaporate without being fully realized.

Community Connections

What made the class particularly appealing to students were its many field trips into the city. Because nearly 180 students were taking six sections of the course, students signed up for three of the four field trips throughout the semester. There were usually about 90 students on each field trip with several chaperones (other teachers, school staff, and myself). School buses transported us from the school into the city leaving at 6 am and returning around 3:30 pm so students could attend after-school jobs, practices, and rehearsals. Though some funding was available for students with financial needs, most were expected to pay between $20–$30 for each trip.

Vernon framed these trips as deliberately interruptive actions that forced students to "cross the line" dividing White and Black, rich and poor. Vernon kept pushing his colleague Tom to eliminate what he called the more "privileged" field trips. For instance, he was pleased in general with how the students behaved for the architectural tour, but criticized it as the most expensive and least inclusive of marginalized perspectives. "I kept wanting to ask about the workers who built the buildings," he tells me in the bus on the way home. "It was good, but architecture just doesn't inspire me like the other trips. I'm thinking next year we should do a tour of home architecture—go to a single-family home, condos, the housing projects." Though some of the field trips were more traditional, many of them were less so.

For example, students read about issues of environmental justice and urban segregation before climbing into kayaks to travel seven miles down a river running through the city. Though they had learned about the historic and current pollution of the river, its frothy foam at the edges and floating pieces of trash viscerally appalled students. We paddled into the industrial district and linked arms as enormous oncoming barges hauling scrap metal and supplies chugged past. The workers stopped to watch the flotilla of suburbanites were all Black and Latino; we were almost all White. The route wove us through this industrial stretch of the river to large warehouses that gave way to expensive riverside condos and then into the heart of the city. Passersby waved to us—this time, mostly White men and women in business suits on cell phones. These social and environmental details did not go unnoticed by the kids as I overheard them discussing the shocking sights and smells of the river.

A similar trip a couple of months later had the kids riding their bikes on a 60-mile loop through the city's historic neighborhoods. They started downtown, then rode into housing projects past abandoned buildings, prison complexes, and all Black faces (some friendly, some not—one little boy, for example, shook his fist at the students and yelled "Get the fuck out of our neighborhood!"). Gradually, evidence of gentrification appeared as we entered neighborhoods with which the kids were more familiar; parks got cleaner, buildings fancier, and people Whiter. Again, kids' conversations with each other ranged from mundane and gossipy to hyper-articulate and inquisitive about the sociology of what they were seeing. Many of them expressed shock and concern that they knew so little about the parts of the city that weren't White or upper/middle class.

One of the students' favorite trips involved a visit to a well-known Latin-American neighborhood in the city. Though not a single student had visited the area before, all had heard about its reputation of crime and poverty. After breakfast of tortillas and eggs at a local café, an elderly man who had immigrated from Mexico years before took them on a tour of a few murals painted on the sides of local buildings. Most of the students were rapt with attention as he described their importance in the community, the political nature of the works, and the ways in which gentrification was jeopardizing their survival. Though I was unable to talk with the guide about what he thought of the field trippers, most of the students expressed great gratitude for this experience; it was the first time many of them had heard a critique of the city's "clean up" efforts or had a Mexican immigrant interact with them from a position of authority and knowledge. On the bus headed for home, I talked with many students about how in awe they were of the art they had seen and how sterile and artificial they felt their community was in comparison.

For the most popular field trip, Vernon organized a student exchange with a predominantly Black public school in the city. West Town students visited Lincoln Academy and were paired with a buddy who showed them around. A few weeks later, the Lincoln students came to West Town and met up with their original buddy for the day. Students were both nervous and excited about being in a school they believed to be so different from theirs. They were shocked at how similar it felt in some ways, though significant differences stuck out to them. The following is an excerpt from my field notes of the discussion that followed their visit to the school.

> Vernon asks for their impressions. One kid says he was shown weed and Vernon sarcastically remarked that such an incident would never happen at West. The kid replied, "Yeah, because we go off campus." Another kid was

shown drugs by his host student who said, "I bet you don't have that at your school!" to which the West Town kid replied, "Yeah, we have the good shit." The class laughs and begins talking with each other about the day. Vernon gets their attention by shouting, "Guys! I want to get your stories," he transitions. "I want us to talk about five things: the teachers and the quality of instruction, the socialization or community there, race, class, and any other general observations like the kids' names or where they're from." One of the students raises his hand and describes how friendly the kids were to each other and to the West High students. They seemed more outgoing, he thought. Fred agreed and described how people came up to him and introduced themselves without hesitation. Taylor concurred and adds that the guys were gentlemen, "They opened the door for me, pulled out my chair." Several of the boys in class groan and laugh while several of the girls agree and talk about how nice it was to be treated that way. "I thought they would give me attitude, but it wasn't like that at all," remarked Taylor. John gets the class to laugh by describing a moment in which "a dude sat down next to me and said, 'There sure are a lot of White kids here today.'" I note that there seems to be much more openness and comfort than usual in talking about race so explicitly. "Who was partners with a White kid?" Vernon asks. John says to Henry, the only Black student in class, that he heard his host was White. The class laughs, including Henry. "Did you talk to any of them about what it's like to be White at that school?" Teegan raises her hand and tells a story that makes me laugh out loud. "In my math class, they kept asking me all these random questions and then this guy asked me my name and said, 'Hey Jessica!' and then later he said, 'Yo, Stacy!' and I responded, 'Do I look like a Stacy?' and he said, 'Well, you look like a White girl.'" The class laughs. Later on in the discussion, Taylor mentions, "I didn't go to a single class where it was one-on-one. Everyone was participating. Like the teacher would ask something and instead of one kid saying something and the teacher saying something back, all the kids would—whoosh! Start talking right away." Vernon re-routes the conversation about the school's social context and the potential reasons for these differences. "Is it because it's a smaller school or is it because of a cultural component?" Side conversations start up. Vernon interrupts them, "Was everyone friendly because you guys were guests?" Fred says yes. "I was trying to be really nice, too, to everybody—it's just kind of like on my mind whereas here I feel like I naturally try to just sit back." A girl challenges this, "I don't think it matters that we were coming or not because they were still nice—they still made the effort." "Is that how you'll be next week?" Vernon asks. Taylor gets particularly animated, "I'm going to bring them into the small cafeteria and I'm scared that no one is going to walk up to them and that our school won't be that friendly at all." Henry speaks up, "When I was sitting down in a sociology class and there was a sub and they didn't listen to him at all, they started talking about all the fights that have happened, like, one kid knocked out his teacher several times—so they do get along, but they still have problems." Vernon connects this comment to the security at the school. "Did you see all that security? The sign that said you will be immediately arrested if you recruit for gangs?" Many of the kids say yes and start to talk about the metal detectors that we had to walk through upon entry. "There was more security, but the staff was a lot more friendly and had a lot more relationships with the students," said Xavier. "Yeah," concurs Taylor who tells a story about her host who would give a special handshake to the security team. "If anyone tried to do that with Bill Cosby, that would never happen." The class starts laughing and many kids say, "Yes!" The class is much more animated than normal. Vernon tries to calm the eruption. "Wait! Wait! Bill Cosby? Who is that—do you mean Howie?" Howard is the head security guard at the school and one of the only Black staff members. "He would never bump fists with a student," says Taylor amidst the comments of many other students. "Why don't we talk about successful African Americans like Howie? Maybe I'm wrong—". Mel cuts him off: "Are you thinking we don't like him because of race? He just knows all the bad kids in a bad way." Vernon gives Mel a skeptical look to indicate that race, indeed, may have something to do with how the kids feel about Howie. Henry again pipes up: "He's my mentor through the Prime Program. We talk about different things in my life. He's helping me with college things, helping me with this class, too—I know him better and he's great." The rest of the class is silent and fairly transfixed. Vernon tells them, "Howie grew up in one of the first Black middle class neighborhoods in the city. His father was a surgeon and friends with Jackie Robinson, he went to a private school, and is a former CEO who is retired and took this job for reasons other than the money. You guys don't know that about him because you've never taken the time to meet him. The whole Bill Cosby thing is really funny because he grew up upper middle class." He switches gears to talk about security again. "So one of the steppers [Black students at West who participate on the step team] got stopped and the guard started really harassing her for not having an ID and then one of the West Town kids got into it with the security on her behalf. How are you going to deal with that when the kid is with you next week?" asks Vernon.

Many of the West Town students grew uncomfortable when thinking about the city students coming to visit, as they were unsure of what kind of reception they would get.

Sure enough, on the end of the second exchange day, there were many incidents that bothered West students. In the reflection after their city school peers left, the students had the most honest and frank discussion about racism at their school that I witnessed throughout the semester. There were many examples of how differently the support staff and other students treated their visitors, differences they attributed to racism. Taylor was especially upset at how a lunch lady had taken off her partner's hat in the cafeteria and shoved it at him without any explanation. "It was so rude. It was racist," she said. At one point during a discussion of interactions between West Black students and the city school's Black students, someone admitted to Vernon that there is a hallway at the school known as "The Jungle" where the handful of Black students who have moved to West Town from the city hang out. Vernon ran with this teachable moment and engaged them in problematizing of such a term, connecting it to the students' earlier reference to Howie as "Bill Cosby."

Ultimately, the students and Vernon lamented not having more time with the students from the city school. Conversations with students in interviews revealed a need for scaffolding students' unpacking of the racism inherent in their school and classroom. In a particularly telling interview, for example, Luna wanted to talk more about the student exchange and ended up telling me about her experiences bumping into the "bitches" in the hall many students called "The Jungle." She explained to me how those Black students were different than other Black students, including her friend and classmate Henry. "Henry is an Oreo," said Luna. "An Oreo?" I asked. She continued.

> He is White on the inside. We have known him for so long. He doesn't offend me because he is not a part of that clique. Just because he is Black everything is directed towards him in class. If you get to know that he is not like that at all. I call him Black Bear. I have gotten past that with him. It is not like every person in that school is like that. It is the people who stand there and play into the stereotype. [Katy: What does it mean to be White on the inside?] He just acts White. He listens to White music. He enjoys hanging out with everybody. I feel like that is not the case with that hall. Black people want to hang out with Black people. We tell Henry, "You are not Black, you are White."

Despite a clear need for more scaffolded attention to the way that students were making sense of what they were experiencing (and, in particular, the ways in which they were constructing race), these field trips did introduce students to facts and figures about social issues from the perspective of marginalized peoples (e.g., José's tour of the murals) and provided opportunities for student reflection and discussion (e.g., the conversation about students' experiences during the school exchanges). Though students did not engage in any formal activism as part of his class, Vernon considered these field trips a form of social action in that his students were crossing a line between their sheltered world and one that is typically framed as violent and dysfunctional.

Though he admirably attempted to connect most topics with their experiences as suburbanites, Vernon seemed most interested in tapping into students' raw emotional responses to these field trips instead of their intellects. Understanding how students felt and eliciting empathy are certainly important, yet relying on them alone can obscure the larger structural forces at work. While many of the West Town High students became much better about examining guilt or sympathy they may have felt, few had opportunities to understand those emotions or reflect on them within a broader sociopolitical/historical context. Luna, for example, enjoyed the student exchange but was unable to draw any parallels to her condemnation of the kids in "The Jungle," to problematize her nicknames for Henry, or to connect what she was seeing to structural and systemic inequalities. Consequently, their ideas for social change and responsibility were limited to individual actions.

In addition, Vernon's considerable teaching talent lay more in planning interesting trips and exposing students to unfamiliar situations than in scaffolding reflections or in-trip activities that could have helped them more formally process what they were feeling. It seemed that students did not have enough time to process their experiences; for example, there were no formal or in-class opportunities to reflect on what they learned or even to think of the city murals in relation to the municipally sponsored historical murals in West Town. After the river trip, Vernon showed the class photographs I had taken and halfheartedly facilitated a KWL chart that, by the end of class, had only the following items: "What I learned: Where Chinatown was located, How to use a kayak, Where places are in relation to the river, All the industry that is still on the river / What I want to learn: How polluted is the river now?" There was no follow up to the last question. Given the pressure to move on with more content and the fact that not all students attended each field trip, the most time they had to reflect on these trips was one class period.

I must note that students explicitly mentioned this freedom Vernon gave them from "typical" written reflections as an example of how they appreciated his treating them like adults. Though weighted, it also seemed that students expected less formal academic work from this elective course. It seems, however, that rich learning opportunities were lost without more official ties between the field trips and their in-class curriculum. Not only could this have allowed students to develop a deeper understanding of what they saw and heard, such reflections in small groups or with partners may have also facilitated an even deeper connection with their peers in class. When I raised this issue with Vernon, he wondered about students' developmental capacity to understand all of the nuances of the trips immediately, the ability to engage deeply in serious issues within a 48-minute class period, and the dangers of hitting too close to home with potentially explosive issues too often. Indeed, the informal conversations students had with each other and with the chaperones while on the trips were important and insightful. Vernon often concluded our conversations with "it's better than nothing"; what he believed he could realistically hope for was to plant seeds for further questioning and action down the road.

This pragmatism also manifested itself in the relatively short duration of these trips that encouraged some students to think of themselves as tourists rather than community members engaged in sustained efforts to build relationships over time. Vernon attributed this to a lack of resources and the simple logistics of organizing field trips for over one hundred teenagers. He expressed concern that these forays into the city, while important as a first step in raising awareness for these students, might also serve to exoticize communities of color and low-income people rather than to position them as complex groups with internal diversity, expertise, and legitimacy. He talked about his teaching as if it were opening a Pandora's Box of issues he wasn't sure he had the time and resources to handle, though positive student responses over the years supported his decision to continue. Encouragingly, the students themselves expressed a desire for more opportunities to forge authentic, sustained connections by suggesting an ongoing action project in the Latin American neighborhood or assigning a semester-long unit project that Lincoln and West students would complete and present together. As the mural tour and the student exchange were in their infancy as field trips, Vernon and the other teachers were in the process of generating ideas for improving them for subsequent iterations of the course. Vernon and I also discussed ways to incorporate art projects and technology into structuring students' reflections and making connections to the readings they otherwise neglected (e.g. a photo essay of the river trip).

In his best moments, Vernon urged his students not simply to step out of the bubble for a deeper appreciation for who and what is on the outside or simply to inspire gratitude for suburbanites' manufactured good fortune, but instead to turn their gaze back upon the bubble itself in order to understand the forces that shape their lives. "Bursting the bubble" should thus not be interpreted simply as suburban kids being nicer to Others or more grateful for the luxury of their surroundings; rather, it can (and should) be about connecting their lives and focusing on the structural conditions that constrain and support particular ways of being for us all. The chapters that follow will further explore how this philosophy manifested itself in Vernon's teaching practices, as well as how his students responded.

Case Two: Social Justice Pedagogy in the City

Liz Johnson

Liz Johnson's classroom is immediately distinguishable from many other teachers' at Kent Academy for its preponderance of crammed-full bookshelves, bumper stickers, flags, political posters, and racks of costumes for historical role plays, all collected over the past ten years of teaching. Chairs and desks for fifteen students (the average size of a class) sit haphazardly in pod formation in the center of the room with different views of the white board and projection screen. Pictures of her children and former advisees crowd her desk. Students constantly pop their heads in to say hello or to discuss a pressing issue with one of the several groups

Liz sponsors (including the student council, a political activism group, and the student newspaper).

When asked to describe Liz, students referred to her as "the personification of Kent" and expressed awe with regards to her intelligence and charisma. She exudes dynamic energy and intellectual curiosity as she speaks in paragraphs with speed and wit. In her early 40s, she is a striking White woman whose typical dress was a casual combination of black pants and a printed top. Though I am a fast walker, I could hardly keep up with her as we moved from one room to another; her stride is strong and purposeful and I found myself initially as intimidated and impressed as the students. There is also a bit of renegade about her; like Vernon, she is not immune to peppering her lectures with typically censored words. She is a "force to be reckoned with," as one student described, and a powerful figure at the school. Aside from the myriad student activities she facilitates, she is also chair of the social-studies department, co-founder of a social-action program for juniors, and teaches several history classes.

Liz grew up in a predominantly White middle-class neighborhood just outside of the city as the daughter of a politically libertarian lawyer and an apolitical homemaker who built a successful finance career after they divorced. For college, Liz attended a private university in the city where she majored in History. After graduation, Liz worked for several years in the publishing industry traveling on junkets for stories about marketing and editing trade journals. On the night she was to return to take a new job in journalism, she ran into an old college friend who was a teacher working with special education students. After hearing about how she had saved one of her student's lives, Liz was overwhelmed by feeling like nothing she had ever done "held a candle" to that. "Literally the light bulb went off. It was an epiphany because I was like, 'That's what I should do.'"

With her friends' encouragement and the support of her mother, Liz moved back home and immediately enrolled in teacher-education classes at a large public university. Frustrated with a lack of rigor in the program's content requirements, she took only what she needed for certification and spent the rest of her time finishing a Masters in History. Her desire to teach in urban public schools evaporated after a difficult student-teaching experience. Though she thoroughly enjoyed her students (mostly low-income kids of color), she was frustrated by the lack of enthusiasm and commitment she observed among the adults. Subsequently, she looked for jobs in "good" suburban schools when she graduated and landed at a large school near West Town to which she commuted from the city.

At first, she felt quite successful in the suburbs. After attending a National Endowment for the Humanities teachers' seminar about constitutional theory, however, she began to think about teaching as "subversive."

> Before that, I had no vision for what I was teaching. I didn't have an historical interpretation, I didn't have any kind of agenda—I was just like, "What kind of cute, cool thing can I come up with today for the students to do with the material?"

Her newfound passion for understanding American history as a struggle for justice alienated her from her colleagues and pushed her to apply to schools she thought might be better environments for her approach. She was thrilled to get hired at Kent, a school she dearly loves and whose mission she wholeheartedly endorses.

> Sometimes I think, like, "Okay. I'm working with rich kids, more or less. Why aren't I out there working with the poor community? "But I'm in love with my school. I'm in love with the resources and the autonomy here. It would be really hard for me to go to an under-resourced school. I just feel like the work that I'm doing—I don't know, I'm trying to—the kids I work with, a lot of them are going to be leaders in some way in some place in the future and if I can kind of sow seeds of fairness and equity in their hearts and minds, it will have a cumulative effect because if somebody doesn't teach the wealthy how to value their fellow man, who is going to? You know what I mean? It has to be done.

Nearly a decade later, she and her husband still live in a neighborhood near Upper North where they raise their two sons, who both attend Kent. Like Vernon, Liz thinks about what it means to be committed to justice while living and teaching in a privileged community.

> Through all these things I've become kind of a radical teacher in the sense that I use my pedagogy to open eyes to injustice. And working with this extraordinarily privileged community—they're getting something that's pretty amazing. It's nothing like my own upbringing. I didn't get anything like this in high school. Nobody talked to me about anything real. Ever. You know, I had to figure it all out for myself. So that's kind of what drives me.

This drive has not gone away over her years at Kent; in fact, it seems to have only intensified Liz's activism and provided space to connect teaching with her involvement in justice work—most notably her activism against the amalgamation of drug policies known as the "Drug War" (what she refers to as "the new Jim Crow").

Modern American History

Liz recommended that I observe both of her sections of Modern American History, a required course for juniors. The students told me that Liz's sections had a reputation for being the most challenging and rigorous in the department. Indeed, the reading load was significant and the system for grading based on a rather complicated formula that included participation, completion of daily work, assignments randomly selected from what students had compiled for each unit, projects, reading quizzes, and formal written assignments. As a former professional journalist, Liz took their writing very seriously and pushed her students to sophisticate their work. In general, students struggled with the workload and Liz's high expectations but expressed gratitude for the challenge as intellectually stimulating and great preparation for college.

Content

There were four major thematic units in the course: "The Legacy of Reconstruction," "Industrialization & Its Consequences," "A Nation of Immigrants," and "Becoming A Super Power." Each of these units examined a topic pertinent to American history (race, class, immigration, and foreign policy) from 1865 to present day. The idea was for students to layer their understanding of each era as they examined the chronology four times through four different lenses. The culmination of each unit was typically a timed essay that posed essential questions from the unit (e.g., "Analyze the New Deal, the Great Society, and Reaganomics in light of today's economic crisis and particularly wealth inequality in America. Whose approach do you think Obama should adopt and why?"). Liz provided copious feedback for students on their essays' writing, originality, and historical accuracy.

Each night, Liz expected students to keep up with upwards of fifteen pages of reading from the primary textbook, *The American People: Creating a Nation and a Society* by historian Gary Nash, and additional readings from a packet unit that included articles and primary source documents. In contrast with the suburban students who largely abandoned the required reading midway through the semester, the majority of Kent students tried mightily to keep up with the workload both for the sake of their grade and out of a genuine interest in the material. Many of the readings directly addressed content explicitly naming White privilege and wealth inequality as significant historical and contemporary social problems. Liz was also committed to including a range of primary sources about these issues: Andrew Carnegie's "Gospel of Wealth," lynching data collected by Ida B. Wells, and Tom Hayden's "Port Huron Statement," to name a few. When presenting facts and figures, she would ask how people at different points of the political spectrum would interpret them. The following vignette is from my field notes during one section's discussion of an excerpt they read from Cornel West's "Race Matters."

> Liz turns on the PowerPoint slide with an overview of West's arguments against White liberals' and conservatives' thinking about Black people. "He talks about how liberals think more government programs can solve racial problems. What's the flaw in that?" she asks. Jane says, "Well, how can government change the way you think?" Liz concurs. "Government can only go so far. Can it really change people's minds? Liberals over-rely on the public sector." She reads from the slide, "Liberals like to relieve their

guilty conscience by supporting funds directed at the 'problem'—Black people. By and large, White people have more access to resources so they support causes and go to fancy dinners for $500 a plate, but West is, like, 'What did you really do? Makes the world go round, but did you really attack racism by going to dinner in a tuxedo?' Fourth one: liberals are reluctant to exercise principled criticism of Black people; they deny them the freedom to err. If you have a critique of the Black community, you run the risk of being called a racist. So liberals clam up—they're scared of being perceived as racists so they silence themselves. And then the last one: Black people need to be 'included' and 'integrated' into 'our' society. Who gets to say what it means to be American? What are your responses to that? Do you think that's a fair characterization of the liberal point of view? Did that third bullet resonate about how liberals solve problem?" Dallas says, "They might just solve a problem not because it's right, but because they feel better about themselves." Liz asks, "So are liberals bad people because they won't get dirty?" Max says, "It's insanely patronizing." Liz asks, "What do you mean?" Cora jumps in, "It's like 'I'm going to do this because I feel bad watching you struggle.' It's not like you're thinking he's struggling— you're thinking, 'I feel bad watching him struggle.' But in a twisted way, at least he's getting help. Obviously, the ends don't justify the means—" "Better to do something than nothing?" Liz interjects. Cora finishes, "In any case, you get some satisfaction for helping people." Dallas joins in: "Liberals have outsourced their benevolence." "Not all liberals think that way," replies Cora. Liz says, "Cornel West thinks this way." Cora continues, "I've never been the oppressed person on the receiving end of the patronizing helping hand, but I could see that. Like, 'Why are you helping me because do you honestly feel bad or want to help me or because you feel bad for me?' There's a difference between feeling that something needs to be done because it's wrong or because I feel bad watching it." Liz asks, "Anybody else on the portrait of the liberals?" Cora adds, "We didn't create the mess, we shouldn't feel guilty about the mess, but it's our duty to help clean it up. This is the situation and now we have to do something about it." "But does that speak to why the beneficiaries of that history should be involved in addressing the inequities? The fact that White people have benefited so much from government policies from the colonies onward—does that history obligate the heirs of that system to address the inadequacies? Things aren't anywhere close to equal and there is rampant unfairness about distribution of resources, the government had its thumb on the scale to tilt it—what's the obligation to do anything about it? Conservatives say not much. Liberals say fix it. What is West saying?" Another girl speaks up: "I would say yes, fix it—not because you feel guilty, but because you have— if it's left up to Blacks to advance themselves, it won't happen because they haven't been given the advances so it would be our responsibility or whoever has been privileged." "Because they're guilty? Resourced?" asks Liz. "Because they're resourced and advantaged," the same girl replies. Cora chimes in: "If we have more people with different perspectives on life and what needs to be done and if we can bring people into the conversation instead of the government and the controlling class, maybe our problems won't get solved—obviously, not immediately—but it will get looked at harder and in a more informed way." Dallas responds, "It's at the point when we've had our thumb on the scale, but now the most we can do is bring it back to balance. So much of the problem in actively bringing it back to balance because now the scale is tipping the other way." Cora challenges him: "I just don't think the scale will tip back to you. Personally, I don't think it's possible for the scale to tip the other way, looking at the history of what happened." Dallas and Cora start debating about the merits of racial quotas in universities. Liz says, "Let me interrupt here to take apart the conservative side. Remember, it's one man, one thinker and you can totally disagree." After some discussion about West's critique of the conservative perspective, Liz says, "Can we acknowledge how weird it is to talk about this without a member of the group we're talking about? We should pay attention to that—there may be other points of view." "That would be awesome," says Dallas. "I think it would be a much more fiery conversation with kids from another neighborhood or kids from another community." "Wasn't there an editorial in the paper about our admissions?" asks Liz. "We're one of the only schools that's talking about this," says Cora. "Like, that guy running for the Senate who was talking to us about privilege and that one freshman asked who he meant by the 'social elite'?" Max reminded them, "He said it was us." Cora added, "A lot of people were pissed off, but I was like, 'He was speaking the truth.'" Liz laughs, "He's not going to get elected to the Senate like that."

Discussions based on primary-source documents or philosophical texts such as West's work were commonplace as students were accustomed to interpreting them as part of their nightly homework. Other resources included segments of documentaries that Liz would pause for brief discussion. For example, during a clip of a film explaining how the repression, consumption, and conformity of the 1950s sowed the seeds of the 1960s revolutions, Liz stopped the film to compare the ways they are being parented to the ways in which the middle-class White children in the film had been reared.

Much of her teaching took place within clear interpretative frames that she shared with her students and expected them to be able to articulate. Liz's students were quite familiar with a series of analytical diagrams, including one that coupled race and class within a pyramid of wealth with a "color line" drawn through the middle to represent the ways in which the wealthy maintained their privilege by promoting race-based policies. Another common interpretive frame was what Liz referred to as the "political spectrum," a horizontal line with four hash marks reading, from left to right, Radical, Liberal, Conservative, Reactionary. When introducing it to the kids she noted that it was "kind of simplistic since other models take more variables into account, but this works for us pretty well." She most frequently returned to this spectrum when presenting students with facts and figures or introducing primary sources, asking how each of the four world-views might interpret them and encouraging students to "weigh" any readings in relation to their own placement on this spectrum. She explicitly supported students' experimentation with these frameworks and defined her classroom as safe space to explore these different ideas in their writing and class commentary.

Students' intellectual command of the facts and figures, however, seemed to be prioritized over any more emotional responses. Opinions, comments, and essay responses were clearly "academic" in nature within the context of a college preparatory education. Though students' empathetic comments or emotions were never explicitly forbidden, neither were they solicited. In written assign-ments especially, students were not asked to personally reflect on their own lives and neighborhoods as much they were asked to take on the role of policy advisors advocating legislation or practice an analytical historian's voice.

Classroom Practices

Liz's classes were packed with planned activities like role plays, structured discus-sions, primary-document analysis, and dense lectures that one student described as a "speeding freight train of information." Despite the density of information she presented, her instruction was rife with opportunities for students to express their opinions and ask questions. She was insistent that kids talk in class and share their ideas with each other. Nearly every class had some discussion, even if it was just "table talk" for a few minutes. One day, when the students were particularly quiet, she told them: "I want to hear from more people. Turn to your neighbor right now—get the lips moving, okay? I've got to rile you guys up a bit today." Liz often played devil's advocate (which typically meant representing a more conservative point of view) to generate conversation. Other class sessions were wholly devoted to soliciting students' voices, whether in the form of a fishbowl conversation about immigration policy or historical role plays for which students would dress as famous figures and respond in character to Liz's discussion prompts. On these days, the room was set up in a circle with Liz sitting on the outside, chiming in only to interrupt a student who might be dominating conversation.

Encouraging students' voice was more prominent than encouraging students to listen, however, whether to each other or to other people. There was one nota-ble exception: an assignment that asked students to interview local activists and to analyze their interviews at the end of the semester. As with the similar assignment at West, students reported being excited about this project but not having enough time to engage with it at the end of the semester. Dylan told me that:

> With any situation where you're fighting for a group of people who don't have a voice, like, use your voice to help others. But I really liked the interview project because I was asking questions, which is using my voice, but I really got to sit back and listen to someone talk about what they did, and I even wished we had just said, "Talk about what you want and we're not going to say anything." Because, like, when kids are offered the chance to ask questions they're like, "Ok I'm going to show-off now." But I wish we had just been like, "You say whatever you want." Because I think that listening is a treat for me, and that when I can do it in such a face-to-face situation with someone who knows so much more about something than I do, that's something that I really haven't had too much of a chance to do without worrying about what I'm going to say next.

As it was the first time this project had been assigned, Liz and the other teachers took notes about ways to improve it the next semester and were excited to develop the project more fully next year. In class, however, students reported feeling much more encouraged to speak than to listen. When asked what she would remember most about class, one student told me:

> Ms. Johnson's class has taught me how powerful it is to speak without a script and how easy it can be when you just have the confidence to do it. It's opened up a lot of opportunities to use that skill other places, because a lot of the things I do for extracurricular stuff are very intertwined with public speaking and being able to work off a cuff instead of off a piece of paper is so important.

Several admitted to wanting to impress Liz, a teacher whose opinion they highly regarded. This desire to be articulate, however, often translated into disdain for other students who seemed less able to voice their opinions. One student told me that:

> I don't really have respect for the other kids in the class. They're just sitting there. You know, they're not interested in reciprocating or giving anything back to the class. And when they do talk, I don't necessarily respect the things that come out of their mouth either.

Another said:

> I feel like some people are just sort of out of it, which is unfortunate. Other people, though, are just really intellectual, or really smart. And some people

I know are afraid to speak, like, not as comfortable with their own ideas so it's harder to speak.

When I asked the quieter students why they did not often talk in class, they told me that they did not want to repeat what others had said. Importantly, several expressed a desire to learn how to be better listeners.

I think we've always been taught like speak up. Like the things that have been said to us are, "Speak up. Don't just let yourself sit in the corner. Don't let yourself be silenced." Which makes us think that's the only way we can succeed: "I have to speak. That's the secret to success." Usually question time comes up and people are like, "I'm going to show off for the teacher. I'm going to show how much I know through this one question that no one's going to remember." And I just thought about like the value of listening is so under-appreciated sometimes. And just being a good listener is a really hard skill. Like by teaching kids how to speak up you are breeding kids who will show well. Like you'll go out into the world and people will be like, "Look at that one. Like, she's got some sense."

In addition to listening to each other, several students specifically articulated how important it was that there was an open exchange of political viewpoints in class. Dylan expressed gratitude for having Jennifer, an outspoken conservative, as a peer.

I think that as opposed to just completely disregarding someone else's views when comparing them to my own, I've changed because now I listen to the other side of the story more so than before. Especially with Jennifer, like I've had a lot of discussions with her about a lot of things and she makes a lot of valid points so now I don't just write her off as some weird conservative, but actually listen to what she has to say.

Paige conveyed a similar sentiment:

Like, inside, I'm like squeezing my pencil when I hear those opinions, but at the same time I like feeling that rage because it grounds what I feel. I don't think I'm going to change her opinion, but I think I'll open her mind up to seeing what I think and understanding what I think. Maybe she's not going to adopt it, but it's good for her and it's good for me, because I know how to react to her and she learns how to react to me. I think that, like, one of the most important things to learn in school is how to understand another person, too. It helps you later in life. Like, if you can understand the people you work with, it's a lot easier, and lot more

fulfilling. And I think that if I, like, understand her even if I don't agree
with her, like, it's a good experience. And I love debating politics. It's fun.

Though she confessed to often feeling frustrated in class and at the school,
Jennifer also recognized the importance of hearing multiple perspectives and
appreciated the moments when Liz incorporated sources that represented a range
of political viewpoints.

Community Connections

In addition to supporting a social-studies curriculum rooted in controversial and
social justice issues with an emphasis on student voice, the school set aside time
and resources to support a "Community Action" program that advocated social
activism. At the urging of Liz and another colleague, the program replaced a more
conventional community-service requirement. All juniors were required to sign
up with one of the action groups led by a teacher volunteer in conjunction with
a social issue to which they themselves are personally committed. These groups'
issues included LGBTQ rights, religious tolerance, drug policy, and women
in prison. Students selected which group they wanted to join and met a few
times each month during a portion of the school day allotted for field trips,
guest speakers, and introductions to assignments that were connected to their
humanities curriculum (e.g., a paper on the marginalization of people affected
by their group's issue in connection with reading *The Scarlet Letter* and a declara-
tion of their group's demands inspired by their reading of the "Port Huron
Statement").

The program's mission is for students to become deeply knowledgeable about
a particular social problem and to engage in direct action that attempts to remedy
it. There was some emphasis on pushing students to consider how their lives were
directly connected to these problems. During the first week of my observations,
for example, Liz and her Community Action students rode a public city bus over
an hour to the other side of town where they toured an alternative-sentencing
boot-camp facility at which drug offenders serve time. The mostly White staff
explained the rules and regulations of the detention center and sang its praises
with statistics of success while the nearly all Black and Latino young men marched
silently in formation in front of us. We walked through the barracks with rows of
bunks and toilets open to the room then filed through the lunchroom where
inmates ate in silence and averted their gaze. The students were horrified and
incredibly uncomfortable. These were their peers age-wise, yet they were living
such clearly incredibly different lives.

During the tour, the students asked tough, pointed questions of the staff
sergeant and exploded into heated debate on the bus home about whether what
they had seen was a step in the right direction toward more sensible drug policy

and a better justice system or continued institutionalized racism.[2] They also debated whether the field trip was appropriate. "I hated it. I felt like I was at a zoo," said one student. Many of the students noted how they had lived in the city their whole lives and had no idea the center existed; none of them knew anyone who had ever been imprisoned. They recognized that the policies that imprisoned these youth had been put into place and supported by adults like their parents who wanted to "keep them safe." As a result, they developed a "Not in My Name" campaign to use when lobbying legislators and petitioning for the legalization of cannabis, the drug for which many of the boot-camp inmates were in prison. In conversations throughout the semester, many students returned to this experience and called it "life-changing" in terms of witnessing firsthand the disparity in their city from those receiving the proverbial short end of the stick.

By bridging the history curriculum with activist groups in which students participated throughout the year, Liz took advantage of ample opportunities to introduce the facts and figures of injustice. Many students became quite dedicated to particular causes or intrigued by certain social issues. The majority of these students, however, most frequently positioned themselves as the knowledgeable members of movements working on behalf of people who could not otherwise work for themselves. Though in the minority, there were also a handful of students who saw the Community Action field trips and the curriculum that complemented them as a way to build their résumé for college applications. Such a mentality could be considered "deficit" and, though not universal, was common enough to be troubling.

In addition, most of the Community Action program's focus was less about listening to the narratives of oppressed peoples and more about listening to the advice and wisdom of movement leaders. The vast majority of students' contact with community members involved people who had grown up in similar privileged circumstances as them and subsequently have chosen lives of service (in several cases, they were Kent alumni or parents). The action projects provided few opportunities to connect students with people from different worlds in authentic, sustained ways. The focus was much more on providing experiences that cultivated students' leadership abilities.

According to Liz, it was logistically easier to meet with leaders whose schedules, locations, and messages so neatly fit with that of the school's. Additionally, the school is competing, in a sense, with many parents' desire for their children to choose a life path that will increase their power and wealth; teachers at Kent feel compelled to counter (or at least to complement) that by presenting them with other options by helping students practice leadership in an activist vein and to meet people who had once been privileged students like them. As these students will very likely end up in positions of power, Liz wanted to influence how they wielded rather than abdicated that power. Lastly, whereas Vernon was willing to bring kids into the city for quick exposures to people different than them, Liz felt too unsure of how those brief encounters might reinforce old thoughts and patterns of behavior. By using her limited time with students to cultivate relationships with activist leaders who embodied similar class and racial privilege, she could avoid the difficulties that arise for both groups when struggling with a significant power differential.

Inherent Tensions and Strategies for Negotiating Them

Taken together, these case studies can be interpreted a variety of ways and are valuable for multiple analyses. My focus here is how these case studies highlight the significant tensions inherent within social justice pedagogy with privileged youth and to examine the strategies that these teachers used to negotiate them. One challenge involves the tension within engaging children from communities of privilege in social justice pedagogy while also preparing them for an elite post-secondary education and positions of power. Another addresses how far teachers attempt to push their social critiques while trying not to indoctrinate or alienate their students. Yet another pits what teachers want to be able to do in their classrooms against the logistical constraints of time and collegial/administrative support.

How did Vernon and Liz balance the expectations of parents, students, colleagues, and administrators while trying to "pry open" students' eyes to injustice? How did they respect and cultivate a multiplicity of perspectives about these issues? How did these two, both members of privileged communities themselves, grapple with their complicity in an unjust system as they simultaneously sought to challenge it? What follows is an overview of three tensions inherent within social justice pedagogy, these teachers' attempts to negotiate them, and more questions that demand more theoretical and empirical research to fully answer.

Tension 1: Balancing College Prep with Social Justice

The first tension embedded within social justice pedagogy for privileged youth concerns the uneasy relationship between preparation for an elite post-secondary education and a vision of social justice calling for socioeconomic inequalities to be interrupted. In other words, most students and their families in privileged communities have certain expectations for how school ought to look and what it ought to do for them—namely, prepare them for entry into and success at competitive colleges and future careers. Social justice teachers in these environments thus must decide how to be strategic about framing their teaching so as to simultaneously meet these expectations while engaging students in content centering marginalized perspectives, democratic classroom practices, and community connections that may call those expectations into question.

Vernon seemed to be deeply conflicted about this and frequently voiced his frustration with traditional expectations of school during interviews with me and in class with his students (e.g., grading, assignments, and having classes in buildings rather than the community). He fundamentally believed that meaningful learning rarely took place in the structure of conventional schooling and thus advocated as much flexibility in class and as many opportunities out-of-class as possible for his students. As a result, he planned few lessons with traditional objectives, formally evaluated very few assignments, and appeared unruffled when students stopped investing much time in class readings or projects. To him, formal assignments, rubrics, and grades interrupted the process of true curiosity and were unable to document the real growth and change happening in students' minds and hearts. Correspondence with former students who took time to express gratitude for their experiences in his class years after the fact confirmed this belief for him.

One way that Vernon managed this was by doing so within the confines of a senior elective. By the time they took his class, the primarily senior group of students had already applied to college and saw their time with Vernon as an experience to be enjoyed rather than something to put on a transcript. Another way was by explicitly pointing out to parents during an open house that his class developed sophisticated skills and knowledge one would need for college. He also noted his academic credentials, cited the success of many of his students, and pointed to the high expectations of the syllabus. Though he painted a picture of a traditional heavy workload, both Vernon and the students largely abandoned the formal "college prep" structure for a more fluid approach. He did, however, continue to talk with his students about the critical thinking and questioning skills he was helping them develop that would benefit them after graduation.

When they compared Vernon with his colleague who taught the other sections, students expressed the belief that while their peers in Tom's class might have "scored better" on tests (which was, incidentally, untrue), Vernon's students "learned more" and would be changed by their experiences rather than just forgetting everything. One unfortunate result of this iteration of social justice pedagogy is that the students framed it as different than "normal" education: while students sang Vernon's praises and claimed the critical, justice-oriented teaching in his class to be important for all students to experience, they also noted that "this kind of teaching wouldn't work in other subjects" and saw it as an exception to the rule rather than a new way to think about schooling writ large.

In comparison with elective-dabbling seniors at West, Liz was teaching a required course for Kent juniors in the throes of ACT/SAT standardized testing who were desperately pushing for the highest grade point possible in preparation for college applications. Of more than a little consequence was the knowledge that parents had serious Ivy League expectations for their children and had been investing heavily in the school to ensure this. Additionally, Liz had a formal leadership role in the department and other positions within the school; the pedagogic choices she made and the commitment to rigor were held up as examples for other teachers to follow.

Liz's strategy for trying to balance the demands of a college preparatory education with a social justice pedagogy was to ground the rigorous reading and writing students did in content and questions related to issues of social injustice. While this approach has strengths, it did little to problematize the fast track to an elite education as a good one on which students inherently deserved to be. Of course no respectable teacher would ever deprive a student of as good a quality education as possible, yet there is something sticky about privileged people studying injustice while participating in institutions that garner them more advantage. Toward the end of the semester, Rachel told me that:

> I think [learning about injustice] can only help because we can reference it and sound really cool for saying it if people recognize it. Otherwise we can help educate people on the things we learned about that maybe they didn't have the opportunity to learn about. Or we just know it and that's great for us. Either way there's no downside to knowledge.

Perhaps the best example of this "stickiness" was one student's response to Liz introducing the concept of hegemony. The word came up in a lecture Liz was giving about wealth inequality in the Gilded Age; as Liz paused to write the word on the board and explain its meaning, Jennifer grabbed her notebook and exclaimed, "Oh! Hegemony—that's a great SAT word. I should write that down!" Rather than expressing curiosity about hegemony as a concept useful for understanding oppressive forms, her interest in learning the word (in a moment of painful irony if ever there was one) stemmed from a desire to enhance her performance on high-stakes tests.

Tension 2: Balancing Multiple Perspectives with Social Critique

The second tension in need of similar untangling involves how far the teachers felt comfortable "pushing" their pedagogy. On the one hand, these teachers consciously chose to work with privileged students to challenge them and serve as a voice critiquing the common sense that renders most injustice invisible. They believed they were carving out important space where, as people to whom their students related and respected, they could shine a light on issues that rarely get "mainstream" attention and model being a voice of justice from within dominant groups. It was impressive to hear some of the conversations in these classrooms, whether it was Liz frankly discussing how the American legal system had been used to further White supremacy or in Vernon facilitating a discussion about racist urban-housing policies. Every single student in the study regardless of background or political identity expressed gratitude for hearing their teachers' social critiques and demonstrated independent thinking about what they saw as the causes and solutions to those problems.

On the other hand, however, both teachers expressed fear of pushing things "too far" and seemed uncertain about where the "line" is between critique and propaganda. Both worried about alienating students and exposing themselves to accusations of indoctrination if they were too forceful with their social critiques. Because West Town High had no clear mission beyond a vague apolitical commitment to "lifelong learning," Vernon's class was the first time the majority of students had ever been exposed to such explicit and candid talk about injustice (particularly in terms of racism and wealth inequality). Consequently, Vernon seemed more comfortable with presenting a single narrative or interpretation of the facts as an important counter to his students' worldviews. He saw his task to raise questions that students had rarely considered and present possible answers they were unlikely to hear elsewhere. He tended to move rather quickly from one topic to the next without much sustained student discussion as a means of provoking students without pushing them too far, and frequently used humor to soften the blow.

Aware of complaints leveled against the school by conservative students about being "marginalized" for their political beliefs, Liz was much more concerned about indoctrination than was Vernon and diligently incorporated readings from a variety of ideological perspectives in an attempt to encourage a "marketplace of ideas" for students to explore. Embedded in her notion of social justice pedagogy was a deep commitment to constructing a democratic classroom where a range of opinions and ideologies could be engaged in the best sense of a liberal education, the foundation of Liz's own personal politics. In addition, because the majority of her students had been at Kent for over a decade and were experienced students of progressive education, many were already familiar with many of the injustices they discussed in Liz's class. Her task, then, was to raise sophisticated questions that challenged students' thinking rather than to promote any one narrative or simply present information that might shock other students. The emphasis of a multiplicity of interpretive frames within which students were expected to be articulate and knowledgeable represents a challenge to them in a way that may not have challenged the West students.

Both teachers wondered how much adolescents should be expected to immediately understand (let alone act on in terms of social activism), especially when the worldviews being presented were markedly different from those in which most students were being raised. In interview conversations with me, they expressed concern about how much new information the students were capable of processing on a developmental level as well as a great deal of compassion for students' nascent stages of a more critical consciousness.

In addition to struggling with how far to push their students in critiquing society, Vernon and Liz struggled with their own desires for the ways in which and to what degree society should change and what that would mean for their own lives. What does it mean for their students to be involved in social justice movements that demand a fundamentally different redistribution of resources and recognition than the status quo from which they benefit? What are the most effective roles for privileged people to play in social movements (allies, leaders, donors, etc.)? How should it be determined which role is most appropriate in a given situation? In terms of developmental psychology, how much can adolescents be expected to do and understand with regards to these issues? And, ultimately, should education explicitly try to interrupt the reproduction of privilege?

In nearly every interview, we butted up against the fundamental (and difficult) question that asked what kind of society we envision as educators and citizens. Did we advocate radical social transformation on a revolutionary scale focused on more equal outcomes or did we promote a more liberal vision of reforming the current system to provide greater opportunities for a wider range of people? Did we want the world to be a more fair meritocracy or a different system altogether? Should we be trying to groom these students to occupy elite colleges and positions of power with a critical, justice-oriented sense of social responsibility or to buck the system completely? How are the ways in which we answer those questions linked to what we would be willing to sacrifice in terms of our own privilege? Though Vernon expressed a more radical vision in relation to Liz's more liberal conceptions, both were remarkably honest about their struggles to make peace with these ideas and tended to leave these questions unanswered in order to focus more on the small steps they could take with their students.

Importantly, there was not a single report among any of the students of feeling pushed too far. In response to my questions about their teachers' viewpoints and teaching styles, and in unsolicited comments related to those topics, many of them voiced their appreciation for these teachers and their belief that schools are an important site for social justice issues to be taught and discussed. One common criterion existed in both of these classrooms that may be the reason that students unanimously rejected accusations of indoctrination that bubbled up on occasion from administrators or concerned parents. In both settings, dissenting views were never shut down; rather, both teachers framed disagreement and diversity of opinion (even with their own ideas) as evidence of critical thinking and curiosity that should be celebrated, cultivated, and challenged.

Tension 3: Balancing Pragmatism with Idealism

In addition to these philosophical knots, social justice pedagogy in communities of privilege poses significant logistical challenges for even the best-intentioned and skilled educators. Though both Vernon and Liz were experienced teachers working in well-resourced schools, this work was not easy for them from a purely technical standpoint. Despite their significant assets, I heard again and again how restricted both teachers felt by a lack of time for planning and enacting this curriculum in responsible ways, a general lack of enthusiasm or understanding from the majority of administrators and colleagues, and a greater need for institutional assistance with regards to systemic issues like scheduling and class sizes that tended to interfere in their plans. In other words, there was a gap between what the teachers wanted to be doing with students and what was logistically feasible.

In terms of collegial and administrative relations, both teachers recognized how important their support was and how infrequently they felt it. Vernon was thrilled when his former students and a politically Left-leaning teacher took over the department chair. A new principal was also very supportive in that he joined Vernon on many of his field trips and endorsed the school visit of historian Howard Zinn. Though he was grateful for this support, he could cite more examples of moments when he had felt alienated and abandoned by his colleagues. When he invited an infamous political figure to visit the school, for instance, the administration caved to "Right-wing" parents who had organized to stop it. He remembered feeling

> Absolutely crushed and kind of alone because nobody else wanted to stick their neck out. And when you stick your neck out, you kind of *are* on your own.

He expressed frustration with colleagues who did not support his approach to teaching, especially the previous department chair who Vernon described as:

> A business professional with socially conservative values and fundamentalist tendencies. He took pictures of my classroom, he stepped in to say the pledge occasionally and thought my classroom should be sanitized and my style should be "objective." This self-professed Christian never showed me where in the Gospels he learned that war or violence is taught by Jesus as an acceptable form to resolve conflict.

To counteract this feeling of being misunderstood or under suspicion, Vernon tried to cultivate relationships with people in the department who had different political beliefs but were still open to his approach to teaching. He seemed to have reluctantly accepted his identity as the department renegade and remained deeply committed to his "radical teaching."

Liz also reported feeling frequently "shut down" by the majority of her peers when proposing new ideas, despite being at a school whose mission was explicitly connected to social justice.

> We've got this amazing mission and I totally believe in the mission and I think we do more than any place I've ever been. We think about it, we try to fulfill it, we do it imperfectly, but it's there. And I guess my frustration— there are just too many people in the building who are not committed to the mission. Why are you working here? Sometimes I feel like the more I push it, the more I get marginalized. I'm like the dolphin nudging

the whale—just gently nudging because if you bump too hard the whale will whack you and you'll be dead.

Mitigating the disillusionment she increasingly felt was the network of social justice activists and friends. Over and over again, she expressed deep gratitude for the few colleagues who were actively involved with her in student groups. Both teachers were committed, life-long members to social movements and groups outside of the school working to advance justice. If they did not feel support at the school, they at least felt that support and had access to shared resources of their peers in the community.

Conclusion

While it may be relatively easy for academics and theorists to envision a "revolutionary critical pedagogy" that calls for an overthrow of a racist, capitalist state in theoretical terms (e.g., McLaren, Martin, Farahmandpur, & Jaramillo, 2004), my time with these teachers in the field convinces me that grappling with how far to push their pedagogy in communities of privilege without alienating their students, being accused of indoctrination, or losing their jobs is an incredibly difficult task. No doubt there were moments when more critical questions could have been raised and students' thinking pushed further in both classrooms, but neither is there doubt that there were powerful moments that students are unlikely to forget. My analysis of these teachers should not be interpreted as a defense of what McLaren, et al. (2004) refer to as a "defanged and sterilized" pedagogy that works "to the advantage of the liberal capitalist state and its bourgeois cadre of educational reformers" (p. 140). Instead, what I hope to have offered in this chapter are poignant portraits of people doing their best to struggle with difficult questions challenging us all so that we may learn to be better teachers and community members ourselves.

5

DID THEY GET IT?

Students' Responses to Social Justice Pedagogy

> We do not grow absolutely, chronologically. We grow sometimes in one
> dimension, and not in another, unevenly. We grow partially. We are relative.
> We are mature in one realm, childish in another. The past, present, and future
> mingle and pull us backward, forward, or fix us in the present. We are made
> of layers, cells, constellations.
>
> *(Nin, 1971, p. 127)*

When I tell family and friends that I study social justice pedagogy with students
in communities of privilege, their first response is typically, "So, do they get it?
Does this kind of teaching work?" Knowing that I sound like the clichéd evasive
professor who answers every query with "That depends" or "It's complicated,"
I tell them these are, in fact, difficult questions to answer. As Gutstein (2003) notes,
"life changes are hard to document, even if one follows them through the
years … and it is difficult to attribute students' development to any particular
events, especially those in school" (p. 69). The way that people learn is extremely
complex and nonlinear. As much as we might want to know if kids "get it," it is
impossible to watch each student during every interaction they have, to peer into
their hearts and minds, or to follow them for an indefinite number of years as they
grow and mature. Someone might seemingly understand some concept in
class, for example, then act in a completely different way outside of school,
and then change their behavior years later when they remembered that lesson.
Did that student "get it"?

What is more feasible to ask (and answer) for this study is how students
responded in class and what that indicates about their capacity for conceptualizing
and acting on their social responsibilities in particular ways. How did the students
at Kent Academy and West Town High respond to Liz and Vernon's efforts to

teach them from a social justice perspective? What were their ideas about their social responsibilities and how did they change throughout the semester? While I cannot say whether or not kids "got it" (which would also imply that there is some definitive "it" for them to "get"), I can say that the students in these classes expressed themselves in ways that confirmed the current literature base warning that social justice pedagogy may backfire with privileged youth. I can also say that they expressed views in line with the desired outcomes of social justice pedagogy (increased awareness, a sense of agency, and the ability to act and critically reflect on those actions). Importantly, tracing these responses can help us to draw conclusions about what kinds of lessons and activities help to cultivate what I describe later in the chapter as "Activist Ally" thinking.

While the previous chapter explored the teachers' philosophies and pedagogical decisions, this chapter shifts to focus on students' perspectives. I analyze students' conceptions of social justice, their feelings of agency, and their ideas about their obligations to others. These can be categorized into four modes of thinking: the Meritocrat, the Benevolent Benefactor, the Resigned, and the Activist Ally. I then discuss these different modes of thinking with attention to how they do and do not support the intended outcomes of social justice pedagogy. In the following chapter, I subsequently investigate which activities seemed to best elicit and encourage such thinking and put forth a modified framework for social justice pedagogy with students in communities of privilege.

Unintended Consequences

As discussed in Chapter 2, the small body of literature examining the effects of social justice pedagogy with privileged students points to the potential for such an approach to produce a series of unintended consequences and, ultimately, to "backfire" in terms of its desired outcomes related to justice-based awareness, agency, and action (e.g., Goodman, 2000b; Curry-Stevens, 2007; Seider, 2008). First, privileged students' awareness of injustice is often limited to abstract knowledge about people experiencing inequalities as a product of individual choices and idiosyncrasies (Leonardo, 2009). Even those students with a more sophisticated awareness of the structural nature of injustice may still, frustratingly, find ways to capitalize on their understandings in order to improve their career marketability rather than as an impetus for critical self-reflection (Goodman, 2000a). Second, privileged students' sense of agency with regards to progressive social change is often thwarted by feelings of anger, guilt, or confusion (Rodriguez, 2000; Rothenberg, 2002; Seider, 2008). Even initially supportive students may revert back to their "original blindness" as the fear generated by examining themselves and the risk of damaging relationships with their social networks appears too great (Heinze, 2008). And, finally, in terms of action, an ethos of charity in the guise of service learning is a common framework in the education of privileged youth rather than building meaningful partnerships with social movements.

Social justice pedagogy so enacted can thus obscure underlying causes of injustice, reify privileged norms, excuse privileged students from critically reflecting on their lives, and reproduce a sense of "Us" and "Them" (Hernandez-Sheets, 2000; Butin, 2007; Choules, 2007; Seider, 2009).

Student Responses

In order to better understand if and when students at West Town High and Kent Academy responded to forms of social justice pedagogy in these unintended and undesirable ways, I traced these students' ideas about the world through interviews, written work, and classroom observations. I wanted to uncover what Howard (2008) calls "ideological operations and frames" that reveal knowledge, values, dispositions, and beliefs that "insulate and regenerate their identity" (p. 214). After coding students' in-class and interview comments, it became clear that there were four distinct modes of thinking which I could use to classify students' ideas about social justice and privilege: the *Meritocrat*, the *Benevolent Benefactor*, the *Resigned*, and the *Activist Ally*. Each mode of thinking can be distinguished by how students interpreted the intended outcomes of social justice pedagogy: a deep and critical *awareness* of injustice, a sense of *agency* to interrupt it, and ideas about what is the best *action* to take with such information and impulses. As I present these different frames, it is important to note that these four "types" do not represent linear stages of development or permanent ways of thinking for students. They are instead a representation for analytical purposes of the range of student comments throughout the semester about privilege, justice, and social responsibility (see Table 5.1).[1]

The Meritocrat

Within this first frame, students' awareness of injustice is idiosyncratic: injustice exists in other parts of the world and happens "over there" to "them." For example, when asked to identify some injustice he knew about, Elliott had trouble thinking of one: "Like, um, Darfur? I don't really know much about it." Brian, "I can't think of any social justice issues off the top of my head. I haven't watched the news in a really long time. I've been really busy." In Meritocratic thinking, any wrongdoing in the world is distant, disconnected to their lives, and can be explained as powerful bad people acting unethically or (more commonly) people making poor decisions that negatively affect their lives. For example, Jennifer told me that, "People either push themselves to get what they want or they give up. Privileges are the results of what you have done."

Students thinking this way often rejected the idea there was a need for feeling empowered since social change is not their responsibility. "Just because you are privileged, it means you have the opportunities to take on those responsibilities, but it doesn't mean you are *obligated* to," said Fred. "There is some responsibility

Table 5.1 Privileged Students' Responses to Social Justice Pedagogy

Mode of thinking	Awareness of injustice	Sense of agency	Taking action
	What is unjust? What causes injustice	*What are my obligations? How likely is change?*	*Given my answers to the previous questions, how should I act?*
Meritocrat	Injustice is "over there" and "back then"; knowledge about injustice is primarily valuable in that it makes someone more marketable	Feel obligated only to their own individual success so as not to waste their privilege; progressive social change (an expansion of rights and equality) should be slow and careful	It is important to be shrewd and realistic in deciding how to act; donate to well-researched causes in order to maximize your contributions
Benevolent Benefactor	Injustice is current and local but only negatively affects the oppressed; knowledge of injustice focused on individual actions of "bad people"	Struggle with guilt, but are hopeful that they can make a difference; progressive social change is inevitable	It is important to be grateful and charitable; donate time and money to charitable causes on a case-by-case basis
Resigned	Sophisticated understanding of injustice as current and local, systemic and individual, and negatively affecting both the oppressed and the oppressor	Feel overwhelmed and cynical about their ability to change society; progressive social change is unlikely or temporary	It is important to do least harm; disconnect from systems that perpetuate injustice and do not waste time on futile political causes
Activist Ally	Sophisticated understanding of injustice as current and local, systemic and individual, and negatively affecting both the oppressed and the oppressor	Feel complicit in systems of injustice and obligated to interrupt it; progressive social change is possible if people organize	It is important to be strategic and cooperative; mobilize your resources in concert with marginalized people

to do the best you can, but that should apply to *everyone*, privileged or not," said Max. Given the way society is organized, a certain amount of injustice is to be expected; according to this mindset, such inequity can actually be beneficial. Emma told me:

> I don't think it's possible there's ever going to be a world where everyone will care and everyone will want to help and no one will be, like, selfish. I don't know, I don't think that could ever happen. And I think it'd be kind of freaky to imagine it. You wouldn't be able to argue with anyone.

According to Max,

> It's like capitalism is the way America's set up. Capitalism is the only way it will work. Don't leave these huge disparities, these huge gaps, but you got to have variety. The population can't thrive without it. Sort of very Darwinian stuff.

Feelings of guilt were rejected outright. Max continued,

> I was born into this, I didn't choose to be like this. I mean my dad worked his ass off, and that's where we ended up. So I didn't choose to be where I am, don't blame me for it.

Luna asked,

> Why should I feel guilty? If you feel guilty, then do something about it. But I don't. Guilt is something you have when you have done something bad and you know it. I think Mr. Sloan feels like we have something we should give them or give back, but we earned them. Other people have the opportunity to earn them, too.

If privileged people do want to get involved, this frame suggests that they ought to keep up the good work they have done which has manifested in their social positions and ought to accrue knowledge about others as a means of becoming more competitive in a globalizing society. In reflecting on how he acted in the world, for example, Max talked about the importance of experiences.

> Carnegie said, like, don't sort of like hide behind your wealth. It turns you into a hollow shell of a man. Like, immerse yourself in music and culture and just everything—immerse yourself in life. And that's what I try to do. I try to just eat like the weird foods, and just sort of immerse myself in every single neighborhood. Sort of live life and see it all.

In addition to experiencing the world (and the "weirdness" of cultures other than your own), one should not be "wasteful" with one's privilege. They should contribute to "deserving" philanthropic causes and take pains to maximize the effectiveness of their investment. According to Jennifer,

> I mean, I know there are brilliant minds out there and if they just utilized like the small things that they were given, I feel like they could make something out of that. Instead of just throwing money at people, we should find ways to, like, start up their motivation.

This approach emphasizes individual, apolitical acts for "deserving" people Fred told me, "like orphans or state systemized people." Overtly political action is a waste of time. Jennifer also told me,

> I didn't want to go out and do picket lines, and I didn't want to go out and yell at people and, like, try to change the world because it's not going to happen. We're like twelve students, and it's just impossible. And I think that for us when we go and interact with the autistic kids, that's like doing them a justice. By just going and hanging out with them and getting them exposure to normal kids.

The individual is primary in this mode of thinking; it is important to be a "good person" who is honest, follows rules, and tries not to depend upon others. The status quo is unproblematic and offers opportunities for those who work hard to rise up through the ranks. According to the Meritocrat, the world will be a more socially just place if and when people take responsibility for their problems and take advantage of the opportunities provided to them.

Students who articulated this schema frequently referenced Andrew Carnegie, the steel baron who espoused a philosophy of philanthropy that came to be known as the Gospel of Wealth. He believed wealth inequality to be beneficial to society, as the consolidation of resources at the top effectively "trickles down" and improves everyone's lives. Meritocrats believe that this works best when the privileged use their power "responsibly" by investing in institutions like libraries and concert halls that provide opportunities for motivated individuals to improve their position in life. Meritocrats thus do not consider themselves to be selfish people; instead, they see themselves as making the world a better place by their individual achievements and feel they should be commended as pragmatists who understand how to most effectively use scarce resources to advance social justice.

The Benevolent Benefactor

In the Benevolent Benefactor mode of thinking, an awareness of injustice is knowledge about current social issues including the environment, wars, gay rights, and racism. It also includes local events. For instance, students referenced the numbers of homeless people in the city and the high rate of incarcerated men of color in their area when asked to identify examples of injustice. Students in this frame of mind talked about these issues as primarily affecting other less fortunate people who are helpless victims of bad luck. Rather than recognizing any systemic dysfunction within the status quo, injustice is a tragic misfortune in the lottery of life. "When you're a person of privilege, it's luck of the draw, you were born into this situation; some people just didn't have that luck when they were born," said Paige. Importantly, the lifestyles of privileged people are not connected to these hardships; rather, luxury represents a haven or escape for those who suffer and often serve as a model towards which those with less should strive.

Benevolent Benefactors tend to distinguish between two kinds of privileged people within this schema: those who take their privilege for granted, and those who are grateful for it. A "good person" within this frame represents the latter and is manifested as someone who appreciates their privilege and engages in charitable acts towards others. "If you know you are privileged, don't shove it in someone's face or get rid of it. Not taking it for granted is a huge responsibility," said Taylor. "Privilege is a gift, kind of, and you can't take too much and you have to accept it. You know, don't overuse it," Patrick told me. Jane advised,

> You can at least be grateful for what you have. Like you're not entitled to it because other people have it a lot worse.

In addition, these students are explicit that "privilege" cannot always be identified by material wealth, but rather is represented by opportunities that a variety of people have. Toward the end of the semester, Taylor told me that,

> People could consider me privileged because I got to West Town and go to a great school and have more education ahead of me. Then again, I could look at someone living in the inner city and they probably have a lot more experiences than I do. … I think some of the city kids [even those who are Black and from low-income families] are more privileged than me because they are more well-rounded or worldly. I am jealous of them for that. I wish I had that opportunity to experience the city in that way.

According to Paige,

> Privilege has something to do with opportunity and that, like, it doesn't necessarily—I think you can be privileged without being extremely affluent. It just so happens that most wealthy people get these privileges or opportunities and sometimes they're wasted, sometimes they're not.

"Bad" privileged people are positioned as materialistic, self-involved, and frivolous.

> I feel like, morally, if you have a privilege, you should treat it as if it's a privilege. Like, don't take advantage of it in a way that it would show that you were ungrateful. But there are some people who kind of feel like their privileges are their rights so they kind of think, "Oh I deserve this. I'm supposed to have this."

In this schema, "bad" privileged people are often vilified for their overtly hostile actions that prevent other people from getting ahead. "*Having* privilege doesn't matter as much as what you *do* with your privilege," said Adam. "That's the line between spoiled and innovative." And Taylor told me that, "the difference between being stuck up and privileged is whether you take advantage of your opportunities."

Rather than working *with* marginalized people, then, the emphasis is on doing things *for* marginalized people that will improve their situation rather transform society. "[Privilege] just, like gives you the opportunity to try to change something when you can because you know that things should be changed," Rachel told me. According to Paige,

> I think it's important for people of privilege to give back to those that don't have privilege. ... I think it's important to show those people—you know, just give them that extra push so they can get to the same point as you, so it's a level playing field for everyone.

According to Emma,

> If you're like well off enough that you don't have to worry about the small things that you're privileged to just have, then you should be focusing on the other things, the larger things you could be helping with instead of the, I don't know, pointless things or materialistic things or popularity you know, that kind of stuff.

Hattie said,

> It's sort of your responsibility to understand that you're very fortunate, very lucky for this to happen to you, and that you can take that power that's been given to you and help someone else who's not as lucky.

Though it recognizes many of the structural issues that may constrain the choices of people within marginalized groups, Benevolent Benefactor thinking assumes such obstacles prevent people from collectively organizing in effective ways, which in turn justifies their own actions as leaders in movements on behalf of people who cannot help themselves.

In this schema, regular volunteerism and community service are considered keys to improving society. These organizing efforts focus on the symptoms rather than the root causes of social problems and locate the problem-solving knowledge within "educated" elite circles. While some reform might be needed, reform that changes the lives of the super-privileged rather than radical change affecting everyone is recommended in this mindset. Rachel asked me,

> Should the cycle of poverty and richness be broken in the first place? Rather than just everything be re-distributed, like, I'd say the middle class to lower-upper class should probably stay where it is, and then the totally wealthy upper-upper class should, like, have to flip-flop.

Whereas Carnegie was a role model for the Meritocrats, several of these students mentioned Oprah Winfrey as a shining example of a justice-oriented privileged citizen who has done much with the privilege she was lucky enough to have. And though they often express some guilt associated with this good fortune, Benevolent Benefactors are fundamentally optimistic that their individual kindness towards others can and will make a difference in those people's lives and improve the world.

The Resigned

This mode of thinking involves a highly sophisticated awareness of the systematic nature of oppression. It is primarily because of this depth and breadth of understanding that students thinking this way seemed to become overwhelmed by the enormity and complexity of social injustice. For example, Mel told me that,

> It's just really shitty that so many of these people are put in a horrible position. These people that don't have the opportunity or resources to rise up, it's because of you know centuries past where, it just seems like you're stuck where you're born. We say we don't have a caste system, but it seems a lot like we do. And you can try to rise in the ranks, but that's a rare success story. We live in a really tilted society.

This thinking frames progressive social change at a fundamental level as unrealistic, however much people may wish it to be otherwise. Efforts to become involved in social movements will have such small effects that it is better to direct energy towards living as consciously as possible by attending to one's own consumer purchases, hobbies, and personal interactions. Society is fundamentally and permanently flawed with no hope for meaningful social change.

Students thinking this way recognized that others may judge them for their ideas and regretted that. Mel confessed that,

> Sometimes I feel sort of helpless. If I told Sloan how I feel about this, he would say I was lazy. It makes me sad, but I've accepted these are things that have been happening and will be happening when I'm dead, too. ... I will do as much as I can to do the right thing in my lifetime, but for me to go out of my way to rewire human nature is completely impossible. ... If you want to talk about oppression and if it's ever going to change, like, I don't think so. ... I remember a friend was in, like, the Gay Straight Alliance for the first two years of her high-school career and any time anyone said "faggot" she'd make a scene about it. But, like, are you kidding? A moment of silence or day of silence just makes gays unheard. You know? No one noticed. ... Face the facts, you're a lousy teenager—there is nothing you're gonna do. Even if you want to make a lousy Facebook group. Fine, someone else knows about it, but the difference is that they just know it's going to end up bad instead of it ending up bad and then they're surprised.

The most consistent and eloquent articulator of this conception of justice-oriented citizenship was Dallas:

> Really, my only feeling of power is in opting out. And because I have certain privileges that other people don't have, or certain connections, I feel as though my ability to opt out is greater. ... I see myself as someone who's just detaching because there's nothing that can be done, and you know that apathy is inexcusable and it doesn't do anything to change the circumstance, but I don't think that it's apathetic in the sense that, like, I can only cast one vote. If I can make my entire life count in every way as a vote, then it's not apathetic and it's not selfish and it's not trying to cast off all the problems. It's being as responsible as I can. I hear the urgency, but I don't feel like it's my duty to redeem the rest of society. It's like I can only be responsible for myself.

Dallas did not consider himself callous or selfish, though he recognized that others might interpret his position this way. In fact, he often took pains to express great compassion for those who are caught in the quagmire of oppression. He did not blame those people for their position and recognized the ways in which institutions systematically constrain them at every turn. Ultimately, he recognized an inability to shed his privilege or use it in any way that would have a lasting positive effect. The best he could do is "unplug" and reject as much of mainstream society as he could by living on its margins.

Perhaps unsurprisingly, the historical figure most frequently referenced in relation to this frame was Henry David Thoreau, whose philosophy, for Resigned thinkers, represents a middle way between a repressive modern culture and a more liberated natural state. They hoped that their opting for a kind of "inaction" would be interpreted as a highly conscious and thoughtful decision that is, in some ways, a form of action in and of itself (though clearly not an unproblematic one).

The Activist Ally

The last frame, the Activist Ally mode of thinking, shares an equally sophisticated awareness of the complexities of injustice as the Resigned, yet without the accompanying sense of cynicism or malaise. When asked for an example of a social injustice, John told me

> Here. I mean, in terms of racial justice—like, we're totally segregated. You know what I mean? As far as a whole school, we're not cohesive. Like, you can tell there's like a White part of the school and then the certain Black part of the school. I just don't understand. Like I don't have a problem sitting with them or—and I feel bad like even saying "them," you know what I mean? I feel like that continues the trend of racism or stereotyping.

He went on to describe what he called the "cycle of richness":

> It's just like one of those cycle things—like, if you get stuck in the cycle of poverty or whatever, it's tough to get out of it. It's the same thing —the cycle of richness. Like you get the advantages, you know people, they set you up—all that. It just keeps going. Like, I know people who are as dumb as can be—total jerks, but you know they're going to end up with a ton of money just because their parents have a ton of money, like, you know what I mean? It's frustrating.

Students thinking this way spoke a lot about how the world is not black and white. Claire told me that,

> You can have people who are successful and are working a ridiculous amount but are stuck in the oppressed and the opposite, too. This is where I am struggling. You have to know more and realize it is not always a straight line. There are grey areas.

They also articulated the subtle nature of how inequalities can be reproduced and to explicitly critique systems that typically go unquestioned. Xavier explained,

> If [the kids from our city exchange] don't pay attention in school and graduate, then they're kind of, like, they're back on the streets and back in

their neighborhood—there are more consequences for them. But if someone here [in West Town], like, most of the time, if someone here drops out or doesn't graduate or does bad they go to community college for a year and a parent takes care of them. They just live at home another year. There's, like, I would say less a sense of urgency here.

Cora explained that, in her mind,

> Capitalism and democracy are somewhat fundamentally incompatible because democracy is about equality and everyone having an equal voice, and capitalism is about rich and poor, and having a gap and there being a differential and people wanting to become rich and the flow of money which is not equal.

This mode of thinking shares a sense of empowered agency with the Benevolent Benefactor, though with very different ends and means in mind. Students recognized their voices as having limits, but also acknowledged their power as privileged people in general and as privileged youth in particular. For example, Cora explained how,

> It's young people fighting for stuff like gay rights because we don't have some of the outdated notions that the older generation has. I think it's always the young people that push movements forward.

At the end of the semester, Hattie told me that,

> On one hand, people want to hear the youth because they don't often speak up, but at the same time they're not taken seriously because they're younger than everyone else; they don't have as much life experience. We're dealing with a lot of issues that are sort of rooted in things that happened decades before we were born, so I feel like we're not taken seriously. If we are educated enough, we're strong enough, we organize well enough—we could be powerful, but at the same time people are reluctant to take youth seriously.

This mode of thinking considers how best to enter into the matrix of efforts to end injustice at both structural and individual levels. Guilt in this frame of mind was not considered to be a productive emotion, though may be an important aspect of learning about injustice. For example, Xavier noted that,

> People who don't feel guilty, like, tend to be more selfish with their possessions or, like, people are just ignorant to everything. ... If they knew what it was like for the people on the other side, they probably would feel guilt, but either they can't comprehend it or they haven't tried.

According to Cora,

> We don't have to feel guilty for the mess that has been created, but it's here now and it's our duty to take care of it. Having been born seventeen years ago, there's no way I could have propagated slavery. But, like, I have at least an obligation to be knowledgeable about the issues. I can't be blind to them because that just begets more ignorance.

And according to Hattie,

> Racism is something we inherited, but we don't realize that we keep widening the gap between economic levels between the races, level of understanding. It's not as obvious because it's more covert. For me, what's important is making people more aware and having people own up to their inner racial, like, tendencies to be stereotypical rather than people feeling guilty.

In their opinions, the world has made steps forward, but it has also regressed; people must be as prepared and vigilant as possible to nudge things in the right direction. At the end of the semester, Cora said,

> People just sort of assume that the right thing will happen because it's supposed to be a just world, but it doesn't because of that assumption and because of that, like, I don't know, I'm like reticent to say that people wouldn't take action if they knew that they had to, because that just is sort of a very bleak view of Americans. But people don't really know, they don't know that like this happens over and over again, without everyone mobilizing things don't happen.

And when Claire talked about alliance, she described it as working with others to make change "as opposed to, 'Here is some money because we pity you and feel so bad.'"

Because Activist Allies have made a connection between the oppression of marginalized groups and their own humanization, fighting injustice is not just about helping Others, but also about improving their own lives. Their privilege, in continual social construction by the complex interaction between structural forces and individual acts, is thus seen as a set of resources to be mobilized in cooperation with the oppressed for the purposes of mutual transformation and societal improvement.

As is evident from the pulled quotes above, Cora was a particularly outspoken advocate for this approach to justice-oriented citizenship and talked at length about the importance of critical self-reflection and deep involvement.

> I think it's easier for people to judge the outside world as opposed to judging themselves. I think that's how the way of the world is. People don't

want to critique themselves, but they want to critique what's going on outside. … I think if you have someone powerful who's trying to affect change, then there's always that sense of, like, who am I to stand up for like the less fortunate when I'm not one of them? Like, do they want me standing up for them? Am I being an ally or have I just inserted myself?

Dylan, another student who expressed more Activist Ally views toward the end of the semester, told me,

I don't like saying "give back" because then it's, like, too linear and one-sided, but I think that if you just, like, "give back" to something you're not involved in at all, like giving back to the community without being back *in* the community, then I think that you just—you waste the opportunity to know people. And I really like knowing people and talking to people and being around people.

Students are quick to point out that any action on behalf of Others should be about more than just giving money since it prevents authentic engagement with other people. Paige noted that,

It doesn't really take much for somebody to write off a check. I know that a lot of the upper-class earners, like my parents, like, they write a check. And that doesn't really help. Maybe that helps the arts, but how much are you really getting involved if you're just writing off a check?

Jane said,

I feel like the people who do the most good are the people who don't just throw their money into and say "Oh I did this." I think it's the people who really care about the issue regardless of how successful they are, and really spend a lot of time focusing on it, and really help make a difference instead of just giving money. I think it's important to spend time because you learn more about the issue, and you really experience it from a firsthand way, I guess.

And Hattie explained that,

Instead of, you know, just donating money or clothes to a shelter, which is important also, we try to lobby state legislators or go interact with people who are living through this.

This mode of thinking thus calls for explicitly political activism to interrupt injustice. Though this may involve some forms of volunteer work or financial donations, it primarily consists of understanding and harnessing the law, govern-ment processes, policies, and other structural forms to address root problems rather than symptoms affecting individuals. Jane explained,

> We're really fighting for everyone's rights and we're fighting to create more of an equal society. And we're not just helping somebody up when they fall, or we're not just helping kids to read, we're helping people fight for proper housing and we're helping people fight for marriage equality, and we're helping people fight for sensible drug policy or, like, support for children if their mother is incarcerated.

Students holding this view of participation recognized that their privilege allowed them access to certain people and resources that could be mobilized on behalf of Others, with whom they work as partners. Listening is thus positioned as one of the most important skills necessary for privileged people planning on participating in social movements. John told me that,

> After awhile, when people start listening to each other and not just know-ing what they know, that's when people start to forgive, and that's when people start to cooperate, but that does take time. … People assume that a kid will learn how to listen over time while you have to sit in class all day. But I think we've always been taught to, like, speak up. Like the things that have been said to us are, "Speak up! Don't just let yourself sit in the corner. Don't let yourself be silenced!" And people are thinking, "Oh, that's the only way I can succeed. I have to speak. I'm going to show off how much I know." And I just think the value of listening is so under-appreciated sometimes. Just being a good listener is a really hard skill. A lot of what we learn is how to use your voice to help others.

This skill is especially important as a means of working with other people from different backgrounds than theirs. John continued:

> I think you have the responsibility to find out what other people want and then take that heavily into account with what you think is right because ultimately if you're doing something for someone and they don't want it done, it's not going to do anything for them, even though you think it's right. You know what I mean? If it's not right to them in their eyes, then it doesn't matter.

Dylan shared a specific example from one of her classmates' projects:

> This girl made a movie about homelessness in the other class and she asked homeless people, like, how did they become homeless? What do you feel

like when someone ignores you on the street? Because we talk about that a lot, about like dehumanization and how that's like the most dire situation of a homeless person. And so she, like, doubly addresses that point by asking them about it.

These students are quick to point out that such interactions are not to be exploitative. At the end of the semester, Rachel emphasized that,

We also have to be sensitive. Like we would like to meet with homeless people, but you can't just go up to people and say, "Hi you're homeless. Tell us about your story." We have to find that balance, like, wanting to educate ourselves based on people's firsthand experiences, but how to be sensitive about that.

Within social movements, people ought to act as allies rather than as their leaders. Hattie said,

Even though it's sort of like a humanitarian thing, it's not really your fight so let them take the reins. Also be understanding. Like, don't just do this because it's a cause. Do it because you feel like it's right and appreciate how important it is to other people you are working alongside with. And so let them take control and help them, just help bolster their cause, not take it over. … Educate yourself, but use the people who are affected as resources, like probably your most valuable resources for understanding instead of treating them like a problem.

One of the benefits of listening is that it prompts critical self-reflection as privileged people struggle to align their beliefs with their actions. Dylan admitted that,

Kent has a lot of very liberal people, or people who think they are liberal, but sometimes there's like a conflict between like the wealth that's here and the liberalism. And sometimes, like, I hear conversations or I see things that come off to me, like, "Wow. You're a very conflicted person, how can you be on both sides of that?" When I see that I'm, like, "Please tell me there's people out there that don't like Laguna Beach and the Real Housewives, who, like, can say confidently they believe the same thing politically that they believe materially."

Ideally, both privileged and marginalized people have much to learn from each other and will be mutually transformed in this process. What this mode of thinking represents is a movement towards a "critical consciousness," which Freire (1973) described as people's capacity to engage in a "legitimately democratic mentality" given its emphasis on root causes of problems rather than symptoms, its attention to the different ways in which all people (themselves included) are dehumanized by injustice, and their focus on committing to issues rather than simply helping individuals.

Mapping Students' Responses

Beyond simply identifying the different modes of thinking represented in both classrooms, it is possible to identify patterns among which students voiced particular frames. By counting the number of times that students expressed a particular viewpoint throughout the semester, for example, I was able to position them on the quadrant of a diagram that corresponds with their general interpretations (see Figure 5.1).[2]

What is immediately noticeable is the diversity of viewpoints among students, though clearly the most common schema was the Benevolent Benefactor. When viewed in tandem with the biographical information of the students, other important dimensions of this data emerge.

First, students' political identities seemed to connect in some way to their ideas about justice, privilege, and social responsibility. Those students who expressed conservative political beliefs gravitated towards the Meritocrat frame, those students who felt unsure about their political affiliations expressed a Benevolent Benefactor frame, those who identified as independents showed affinity for Resigned thinking, and those with strong liberal views tended to articulate more of an Activist Ally frame.

Second, students' cognitive maps seem related to their "privileged" status in terms of class. For the most part, Vernon's White students who openly identified

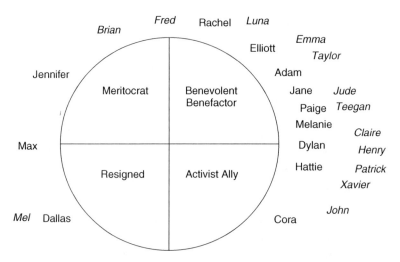

FIGURE 5.1 Privileged Students' Interpretations of Justice-Oriented Citizenship.

as working class (e.g., Xavier, Patrick) and Liz's student from the middle class (e.g., Cora) tended to espouse Activist Ally viewpoints more strongly and more frequently than their more affluent peers. In addition, self-identified students of color also tended to exhibit increasing Activist Ally thinking throughout the semester (e.g., Henry, Melanie). None of these students expressed Meritocratic views. In other words, the weaker their ties to traditionally "privileged" racial and economic groups, the more likely it seemed that students were to express justice-oriented conceptions of citizenship that aligned with social justice pedagogy.[3] With such a small sample of students, however, I hesitate to draw any broad conclusions about this pattern and encourage more investigation with other students in other contexts.

Implications for Classrooms

Understanding privileged students' varying conceptions of the nature of injustice (awareness), their sense of agency to do something about it (agency), and their related social obligations (action) raises several critical points about social justice pedagogy with these youth. First, it is important to note that rather than simply "backfiring," students' responses were much more complex than the current literature suggests. Though all students claimed to be "justice-oriented" whether they articulated Meritocrat, Benevolent Benefactor, or Resigned points of view, they did not seem to recognize these views as incompatible with the demands of justice. It seems that students mapped what they were learning about social justice onto a deeply embedded logic of privilege that tends to naturalize hierarchies and disembody injustices from individual and structural forms of supremacy. These student responses demonstrate how difficult it is to challenge deeply-held worldviews produced, supported, and made invisible by the systems that privilege them—even when people want to and think that they are working against injustice.

This phenomenon reminds me of a passage from Paolo Freire's (2000) *Pedagogy of the Oppressed* where he describes people who "cease to be exploiters or indifferent spectators or simply the heirs of exploitation and move to the side of the exploited" (p. 60). He says,

> they almost always bring with them the marks of their origin: their prejudices and their deformations, which include a lack of confidence in the people's ability to think, to want, and to know. Accordingly, these adherents to the people's cause constantly run the risk of falling into a type of generosity as malefic as that of the oppressors. The generosity of the oppressors is nourished by an unjust order, which must be maintained in order to justify that generosity. Our converts, on the other hand, truly desire to transform the unjust order; but because of their background they believe that they must be the executors of the transformation. They talk about the

people, but they do not trust them; and trusting the people is the indispensable precondition for revolutionary change.

(p. 60)

In order to avoid supporting the "malefic generosity" against which Freire warns, it is thus absolutely essential that teachers identify how students are interpreting justice and their related social obligations as privileged youth.

Critical Questions

To do this, there are several important questions for teachers to think about on their own and with their students. These are questions I asked in interviews and that came up in classroom discussions, both as planned and spontaneous prompts. How teachers and students answer them provides a guide for what materials and experiences may challenge them in productive ways and serves as a reflective tool for teachers to know how their students are interpreting their pedagogic decisions.[4]

What Power Do You Have? When and Where? Why?

The first few questions represent inquiry into the nature of privilege as power and its relationship to justice: What power do you have? When and where do you have power? Why do you have it? These questions ask students to think about themselves in relation to the world and to identify explanations for how these positions have been constructed and are maintained. In terms of the modes of thinking, the Meritocrat might answer this question by pointing to their family's hard work, the Benevolent Benefactor may credit luck, the Resigned because of a long-standing caste system, and the Activist Ally because of people's choices as constrained by historical and contemporary structural inequities. Addressing explanations for why these power differentials exist are the first step in any social justice pedagogy with privileged students.

What Do You Do with Your Power?

The second question asks students to think about their actions: What do we do with this power? For the vast majority of students in these case studies, this was a question they wanted to ask and one that the teachers raised in class and on field trips. The most typical answer from students and teachers was that of the Benevolent Benefactor: express gratitude for that power and use it to do things for other people who are less lucky. Other responses included the Meritocrat's directive to use power in prudent ways for those who deserve it and the Resigned to do least harm by unplugging from society. By explicitly asking this question of historical and current cases, teachers have an opportunity to present students with examples of what an Activist Ally would do by using power to act *with* others in ways that challenge their own positions as privileged people.

How Should the Distribution of Power Change?

Last but not least, the final question, and perhaps the most explosive given its potentially radical undertones, is whether or not the distribution of power should change and, if so, in what ways? I raised this question towards the end of each semester in interviews with students and teachers; even the most radical were reluctant to say that society should be completely reorganized. This was by far the most uncomfortable question to ask and, from the shifting in their seats and tones of voice, the most uncomfortable to answer. Yet it is one that begs to be explored within a social justice class with students from communities of privilege. According to Goodman (2000b), "We need to provide visions and alternatives that change people's ways of thinking, acting, and behaving. ... In this sense, the aim is not to change roles or change who has power but to change the very nature of the system" (pp. 195–196).

What Justice Demands

What power do we have? When and where do we have it? Why do we have that power? What do we do with that power? In what ways should that power be more justly distributed? Asking these questions opens up space for all students to examine the sophisticated ways in which different aspects of their identity intersects with historical and structural realities; for example, to be White and working class in a wealthy community is different than being White and wealthy in that same community. Family structure, religion, gender, sexual orientation, physical ability, citizenship status, language: all of these aspects of a student's identity present rich opportunities to investigate how power does and should operate in society.

That students will come to different conclusions about these questions is not a bad thing; these are the fundamental questions that all members of a thick and healthy democracy should be prepared to ask and answer. In order to encourage a social justice education that is not indoctrinatory we also need to respect the plurality of ways in which individuals can be politically active. The rich ideological and philosophical diversity shown to exist in even quite homogeneous classrooms like those of Liz and Vernon's is quite valuable in that it is intellectually stimulating and demonstrates a diversity of opinions about justice, citizenship, and privilege that exist in our society writ large. Though it may be easy to dismiss the Meritocratic mindset as selfish or the Benevolent Benefactors as naïve or the Resigned as apathetic, it is crucial to note that students thinking within these frames certainly do not see themselves that way; they care about the world and believe the best way to advance justice is by maximizing their monetary donations, engaging in charitable acts, or living the most conscientious life they can. These are core beliefs with which any good social justice teacher can connect.

Yet while one cannot ignore the important and complicated role that such philanthropic or individual acts play in social movements today, educators must be willing to confront (with each other and with their students) the ways in which such beliefs mask oppressive forms. For instance, the Meritocrat's and the Benevolent Benefactor's awareness of injustice is limited to abstract knowledge and a deficit view of the Other rather than any sort of deeper understanding. In terms of agency, these frames focus solely on "bad" individuals rather than acknowledging structural forces at work or implicating their own actions. In addition, the Meritocrat, Benevolent Benefactor, and Resigned all dismiss collective action (and particularly the action of youth) as unnecessary or impractical. Under the guise of "social justice," these schemas thus lead to the framing of problems and solutions that are more likely to reproduce inequality than interrupt it.

For social justice pedagogy intent upon facilitating the development of justice-oriented citizens with a deep understanding of systemic injustices, a sense of agency that is empowered and critically self-reflective, and the ability to mobilize their resources in order to act in concert with others, the Activist Ally is clearly the most desirable schema. Of course, even the best teachers and students will struggle to embrace an Activist Ally conception of citizenship in all situations. Given the complexities and challenges for people privileged by oppression when they engage in social justice work, it is likely that even dedicated allies will find themselves at times operating within other frames and supporting the reproduction of hierarchies. This schema is simply the most aligned with the desired outcomes of social justice pedagogy and, as such, is an important guiding idea around which curriculum can be designed and assessed (more about this in Chapter 6).

Though the literature cautions that engaging students from privileged communities in social justice pedagogy may be counterproductive and engender student resistance, the findings described here point to a more complex set of responses that illustrate students grappling with what it means to be a "justice-oriented citizen" in markedly different ways. For teachers committed to social justice pedagogy, understanding students' ideas about privilege and justice can help to identify moments when their lessons are being taken up in superficial or unintended ways, particularly with regards to students whose thinking and actions may initially seem to align with justice-oriented goals. The cognitive schemas identified here are most useful as a reflective tool for privileged students and their teachers to explicitly think about the very different conceptions of what it means to be a "justice-oriented" privileged person and to more effectively advocate for community members who will understand the systemic nature of injustice, acknowledge their complicity in these systems, feel a sense of empowered agency to make a change, and mobilize their resources as a way to act in concert with others to further justice.

6

EYES PRIED OPEN

A Framework for Educating Activist Allies

For teachers working with privileged students right now, the most pressing questions they are likely to have at the end of any volume of educational research are those related to everyday classroom practices and how to improve them. In other words, what does all of this mean for their teaching on Monday? Relative to this book, these questions might include: which philosophy of teaching (bursting the bubble or disturbing the comfortable) is most applicable to their unique contexts? How do they know which mode of thinking is shaping their students's conceptions of justice and social obligations? Which classroom practices are to be avoided given that they promote Meritocrat, Benevolent Benefactor, and Resigned modes of thinking? Which support the development of Activist Ally frames and should thus be embraced?

This final chapter represents my attempt to answer such questions by proposing a framework for educating activist allies that I hope will be helpful in guiding the development and assessment of social justice pedagogy with privileged youth as teachers work to pry open their eyes to injustice around them and their related social obligations. First, I provide a description of the framework with attention to its theoretical roots. Next, I examine examples from Vernon Sloan and Liz Johnson's classroom practices in relation to this framework in order to understand its strengths and weaknesses. Lastly, I make a case for why this approach holds promise for educators working in classrooms right now and suggest several concrete ways that teachers can implement this framework in their classrooms.

An important note before we begin: the idea of "prying" in this chapter's title is not meant to endorse a forceful act perpetrated against a student's will. Often, prying is required not because we wish to keep something closed, but because we are unsure of how to open it or because an outside force is working to keep it sealed. The use of "prying" here is thus intended to be an honest description of the difficult and sometimes painful process for people in privileged communities to learn about injustice, to become aware of their connections to it, and to engage in thoughtful ways to interrupt it.

Educating Activist Allies

The Educating Activist Allies model is organized by three categories: *content, classroom practices,* and *community connections.* For those readers paying close attention, these are the same categories I used to define social justice pedagogy in Chapter 2. For lack of a better term, the "conventional" approach to social-justice pedagogy described there includes curriculum content that is inclusive of multiple perspectives grounded in an assumption that systemic, institutional oppression exists; democratic classroom practices where students' voices are valued and lives reflected with opportunities to engage in individual critical self-reflection; and practice participating in collective action within multiple communities in order to build a less oppressive society. While there is little in this definition that would raise red flags for most supporters of social justice pedagogy, we have seen from Chapters 2 and 5 that its enactment does not ensure that students will automatically adopt the hoped-for dispositions, knowledge, and skills. These efforts, in fact, may "backfire" with privileged youth by supporting thin conceptions of justice and weak social obligations.

After identifying the modes of thinking that emerged in Vernon Sloan and Liz Johnson's classrooms (the Meritocrat, the Benevolent Benefactor, the Resigned, and the Activist Ally), I thus tried to tease apart the common criteria among lessons that elicited more of an Activist Ally mode of thinking from those that did not. What I found was that those activities emphasizing personal connections to injustice, critical self-reflection, listening, and relationship-building over time with people from marginalized groups tended to elicit more Activist Ally thinking than did those activities that emphasized abstract knowledge, emotional disconnection, intellectual opining, and unidirectional service projects or short-term field trips. When arranged along the lines of content, classroom practices, and community connections, this latter set of activities make up what I call a *conventional* model of social justice pedagogy while the former makes up the model of *Educating Activist Allies* (see Table 6.1). Given that it was developed after my research ended as a way to make sense of the data I collected, the teachers with whom I worked were unable to consciously implement this framework to "test" its efficacy. For now, this model remains theoretical, though it is rooted in analysis of students' responses to a variety of activities and lessons.

Rather than presenting issues of injustice as primarily historical, abstract, or attributable to individual actions, teachers using the Educating Activist Allies framework ask students to make connections between what they are learning about long-standing structural inequalities with contemporary issues and their daily lives. They also encourage students to critically reflect on this information in

TABLE 6.1. Comparison of Conventional Social Justice Pedagogy with Educating Activist Allies

	Conventional Social Justice Pedagogy	Educating Activist Allies
CONTENT	Teachers present students with content inclusive of multiple perspectives as well as the facts and figures of abstract social justice issues; focus on intellectual analysis of issues; assign blame for acts of injustice on corrupt individuals	Teachers present students with content inclusive of multiple perspectives as well as facts and figures of social justice issues that are explicitly connected to students' daily lives; engage students' emotions and intellects; contextualize injustices within individual acts and structural forces that reproduce injustice
CLASSROOM PRACTICES	The classroom is a student-centered space with opportunities for students to engage in critical self-reflection, articulation of their opinions, and discussion of social issues	The classroom is a student-(de)centered space with an emphasis on listening to the stories of oppressed people from their own voices and perspectives; students and teachers are held accountable for marginalization happening in their own school and classroom
COMMUNITY CONNECTIONS	Students engage in community service or civic action that focuses on the symptoms of social issues; teachers prepare and encourage them to be leaders of social movements	Students engage in building relationships with marginalized people that work to transform all parties as well as the institutions of society; teachers prepare students to work as partners in fighting for justice
LIKELY OUTCOMES	Students may… • Develop knowledge of injustice, focus on individual acts • Deny complicity in injustice • Feel disconnected, overwhelmed, guilty, or victimized • Refuse to participate in social action or choose to participate by doing things for other people as a savior figure • Maintain distance from or briefly interact with marginalized people • Cultivate unilateral power relations between them and others	Students may… • Develop sophisticated understanding of injustice, focus on structural forces and individual acts • Accept complicity in injustice regardless of intentions • Feel empowered to address individual and structural injustice • Choose to participate in social action as an ally who mobilizes resources in coordination with efforts already underway • Build dialogic relationships with marginalized people that develop over time

both intellectual and emotional ways. With regards to democratic classroom practices, teachers emphasize soliciting and listening to the stories of marginalized people over articulating one's own opinions. They also stress respectful listening among classmates and attending to injustices at the most local levels of the classroom and school. Lastly, in terms of action, teachers encourage students to accept social responsibility in relation to injustice and to learn how to mobilize their resources as allies working within social movements. An "ally" here is to be taken in the same vein as Freire's (2000) "radical" who,

> committed to human liberation, does not become the prisoner of a "circle of certainty" within which reality is also imprisoned. On the contrary, the more radical the person is, the more fully he or she enters into reality so that, knowing it better, he or she can better transform it. This individual is not afraid to confront, to listen, to see the world unveiled. This person is not afraid to meet the people or to enter into dialogue with them. This person does not consider himself or herself the proprietor of history or of all people, or the liberator of the oppressed; but he or she does commit himself or herself, within history, to fight at their side.
>
> *(p. 39)*

This is in contrast with a conventional approach to social justice pedagogy with privileged youth that may encourage students to assume leadership positions in unidirectional service projects or to use their burgeoning critical awareness of the world as a kind of cultural capital to garner more privilege.

Political Compassion

Though I developed the framework for the Educating Activist Allies model of social justice pedagogy primarily through the analysis of data from Vernon and Liz's classrooms, the work of several scholars influenced my thinking: Applebaum's (2007) model of White complicity, Edwards' (2006) aspiring social justice-ally identity development, and Westheimer & Kahne's (2004) justice-oriented citizenship. For those interested in engaging in social justice pedagogy with privileged youth, I highly recommend that each of these authors' writing be added to their reading lists. When I was a classroom teacher, reading philosophy and theory could seem like a distraction from more practical work, yet I was always tremendously inspired to rethink what I was doing and why when I read a particularly powerful or provocative piece. In this study, the primary idea inspiring me to think differently about the data I was collecting and analyzing was O'Connell's (2009) theory of *political compassion*.

In trying to build a framework for social justice teaching and learning that elicits the intended student responses of awareness, agency, and action, O'Connell's conception of political compassion is quite useful. Though her philosophizing is rooted in secular scholarship (most notably the political philosophy of Martha Nussbaum), O'Connell is a theologian urging North American Christians to reexamine compassion in an age of globalization. She first identifies several values perpetuated by privileged groups within a "particularly American" context: individualism, autonomy, self-sufficiency, consumerism, Whiteness, and "bourgeois" Christianity. These values are at the root of privileged people creating categories of deserving and undeserving people, attending to the experiences of Others out of voyeuristic curiosity, ignoring the structural causes of individuals' suffering, condemning vulnerability, becoming trapped in disempowering cycles of charity, placing the onus for social change on those who suffer, and emphasizing personal sin rather than collective concern with social suffering.

These actions represent a "thin" approach to social justice and parallel the ideas that Meritocrats, Benevolent Benefactors, and Resigned thinkers have about why injustice exists and what they are obligated to do about it as privileged people. Instead of these weak and ultimately destructive forms of compassion, O'Connell promotes what I would call an Activist Ally mindset that is "able to see, interpret, and respond to the type of dehumanizing suffering that social disasters create" (p. 149). Seeing, the first element in O'Connell's theory of political compassion, involves a student's ability to *perceive social disasters through relational anthropology*. In other words, privileged people must perceive those who suffer as valuable human beings operating within sociohistorical contexts rather than reducing their afflictions to abstract, ahistorical statistics. Before interpreting social issues or beginning to act in any way, privileged people must also contextualize their own perceptions of the world and try to see themselves as marginalized people see them.

After adjusting perceptions of injustice through this "de-centered self-awareness," the second element of political compassion is to *interpret social disasters through interruptions*. In this stage, privileged people first ask why people suffer as they do (rather than what can be done to help), listen to their stories as starting places for analysis, and incorporate emotion as well as reason into their understanding of the situation. Essential in this process is making space for the memories and narratives of marginalized people. This is an attempt to remedy what Fricker (2007) calls *testimonial injustice*, which occurs when a listener with power fails to properly recognize an individual or refuses to take another's claim seriously because of some type of prejudice like racism or classism. Because members of the privileged class are more likely to see their privileges as either legitimately earned or unattached to structural problems, they are less likely to recognize the suffering of others and how it is likely due to systematic disadvantages rather than individual failings (Applebaum, 2010; Khan, 2011). O'Connell (2009) calls these opportunities to listen "humble encounters" and notes how they might present themselves in a variety of ways including informal conversations, formal interviews, popular music, and the visual and performing arts.

This leads to the third phase of "political compassion": *transforming social disasters through empowerment, humility, and solidarity.* Through "storytelling, deep and humble listening, engaging all of our senses in understanding one another's situations, dialogues about common concerns, and brainstorming about ways to create alternatives to the way things are" (p. 177), three forms of transformation take place: the transformation of marginalized people, the transformation of privileged people, and the transformation of society's structures and institutions. First, those who are typically victimized by conventional forms of compassion are empowered by the opportunity to "determine their own plan for flourishing and to challenge notions of flourishing held by the wider community" (p. 172). Next, those whose privilege is reinforced by conventional forms of compassion develop self-critical humility, asymmetrical relationships with marginalized people, and new worldviews crafted by listening to the narratives of those who suffer.[1] Lastly, the wider social reality can be transformed by replacing the values of individualism, self-sufficiency, and Whiteness with the values of relationality, vulnerability, and humanness in order to rethink and remake the organization of social spaces and institutions.

O'Connell (2009) concludes her argument for political compassion with a description of justice as a "way of being" in the world:

> We move beyond *thinking about* justice in terms of its classic definition of "giving others their due," which sustains a competitive relationality among persons, and toward *being about* justice, which sustains an empowering and corporate resolve to "do what is ours to do."
>
> *(p. 202)*

What O'Connell calls political compassion is a coherent and thoughtful vision that challenges conventional notions of compassion that tend to reinforce rather than interrupt the unjust status quo. Her development of a framework helping privileged people to see, interpret, and respond to injustice is clearly applicable to educational settings and is woven into my Educating Activist Allies framework.

What Does This Look Like in Action?

Though Vernon Sloan and Liz Johnson were not purposefully trying to engage in an Educating Activist Allies model given that this was developed as a result of analyzing their practices after the fact, examining their pedagogic choices makes it clear that those that fit within this model tended to produce student responses more in line with their desired outcomes than did those activities and lessons that fit better within a conventional model of social justice pedagogy. Though there are many examples I could pull from the case studies in Chapter 4 (and encourage readers to revisit those case studies with this new framework in mind), I now present a particularly powerful moment from each teacher's class to examine through an Educating Activist Allies lens in an attempt to better understand the feasibility and effectiveness of this new approach to social justice pedagogy.

The Scummy-Looking Girl

In class, on assignments, and during field trips, students in Vernon's class were generally praised for their articulate speech, hard-hitting questions, and opinions rather than for listening to marginalized voices—or to each other. In one-on-one conversations, some of the quieter students confessed to being intimidated by their peers. Even more noted that they spoke little in class because they did not want to say something simply for the sake of having their voices heard. In contrast, the more talkative kids described their quieter peers as ignorant, uncaring, or stupid. For example, Mel expressed his frustration with one of his peers in an interview with me halfway through the semester. Despite his own critiques of the suburban ideal and his self-reflection about not fitting in, he called one girl out as "dead weight" in the class without knowing her name or much about her. When I asked him to identify her, he told me:

> That one girl is kind of scummy looking. I don't know what's wrong with her. It's funny that she's in Sloan's class. I think he knows and doesn't care to challenge her or maybe he just completely overlooks it, but she has one of the most insightful teachers in school and she's a total idiot about being open-minded, like, she has the worst opinions.

When asked to describe her classmates during an interview with me, Luna, the girl Mel had been talking about, broke into tears and confessed how intimidated she was by the boy who had (unbeknownst to her) critiqued her. When I shared these findings with Vernon and pointed out how much more frequently boys spoke in his class, he immediately made a seating chart and told the students the next day why he was making the change.

> Some of you have been too comfortable, sitting in cliques. I consider this a community and so I've forcefully integrated you like Brown versus Board should have integrated the city. I also want to make another point that was really interesting to me—someone pointed this out. I would like to hear other voices in this classroom. There is overwhelming testosterone—it's poisonous. Generally, it does horrible things.

Afterwards, several students told me how different the classroom felt. There was overwhelming support for what students identified as an "open forum" where they could hear viewpoints different than their own:

It's better. The cliques don't sit next to each other. There is more listening.

One person who I never heard speak before, even she talks every now and then. I like to hear everyone's opinion. I always hear Mel, so I like to hear the quiet ones, too. I think they are comfortable because they are not going to be attacked. You can't be wrong with your opinions. Everyone can somehow relate to the topics we talk about here, where in other classes that is not always the case.

Before, I knew Mel and those guys got into trouble. I thought they would come in class and not care or contribute, but I realized that they have more to say than anyone in class. I got to hear their sides of the stories. All of their thoughts and opinions—they helped in class and with my views. Sitting in class with all of these different kids and a teacher who treats everyone as equals and understands and encourages them to share their thoughts—I think it helps that the class was an open forum to talk.

The dynamics of the classroom—it's so different than every other class I am in. We have different viewpoints. The atmosphere is good because there are a lot of different opinions.

Though there are many ways that Vernon could have responded to the stories I shared with him that would fit within an Educating Activist Allies model, his decision to make a new seating chart and to be frank with the class about why he was doing so is an example of attending to the power dynamics in his classroom and explicitly connecting it to the issues they were studying. As the Educating Activist Allies model requires, his more powerful students were "de-centered" and asked to be better listeners to each other, as well as to take responsibility for inequalities that had been happening within their classroom. The result was that students participated more frequently in class discussions, felt safer expressing their views, and voiced an appreciation for the range of perspectives more than they did before. In short, it was a more democratic classroom space that reflected the content they were learning and seemed to produce the desired outcomes as outlined by the model. It was also a reminder to Vernon that *how* you teach and *where* you teach can powerfully undermine or reinforce *what* you teach.

A Bridge to the World You're Inheriting

The following vignette comes from my field notes toward the end of the semester; I chose it both for its normalcy in relation to Liz's other class sessions I observed as well as its exemplifying the skill with which she tried to encourage deep critical thinking and reflection by connecting primary sources with students' lived experiences—an essential component of the content component of Educating

Activist Allies. For homework that day, students had read the "Port Huron Statement" (PHS) written by Tom Hayden.

Liz says, "Today's the day we talk about what the PHS is saying about what they are inheriting and we make the bridge to the world you're inheriting—not just you as students, but as members of your Community Action group. You've been exposed to things you didn't know about before—would you agree that you've learned a lot? I know my group has—they didn't know anything about drug policy. They don't necessarily have answers, but they know a lot more than they knew about before." She draws a sin curve on the board with dates at the troughs and peaks spanning from 1900 to 2010. "There's a pattern you can observe and dispute—a sin curve of reform movements throughout the 20th century." Everyone is in class sitting in a large circle. Liz notes that the PHS comes right before the peak of the 1960s reform movements. She puts "2010?" at the final peak but poses a question to the class: "Are we on the way up? Or are we on the way down?" Jane's hand is up. Liz draws a T-chart on the board—"Old Left"/"New Left". She also draws the political spectrum on the board. "They're calling themselves the New Left because they want to distinguish themselves from the Old Left." Dylan suggests she add FDR [Franklin Delano Roosevelt]. "He's more of a liberal," says Liz. "We're talking about the radicals. You can name one." Someone says Eugene Debs. Dylan suggests the Socialist Party. Liz adds the IWW [Industrial Workers of the World]. Paige asks if the AFL would go in there. Liz explains how the IWW took Black members, immigrants, unskilled workers, etc. She categorizes the AFL [American Federation of Labor] as a professional union that didn't want to deal with the issues of the people "below." "How come these groups are no longer dominant political forces?" Sarah suggests the Red Scares. Liz reminds them of the Palmer Raids. "Some of these are old-school violent revolutionaries. Is the PHS calling for violence? The Communist Manifesto is about 'rise up, break your chains, workers of the world unite'—these guys are talking about participatory democracy and retaking institutions, not by storming the gates or coups or barricading the streets, but by what? What is it?" "It's more inclusive," says Melanie. "Less politics, more government," says Dylan. "The advantage that they have is their youth—they didn't experience McCarthy themselves. They think they can break away from it," explains Liz. Jane notices, "It's kind of like they've inherited so many problems that they have to move towards a more progressive, democratic society and this is their way of doing it." "And what is their way? What does a more democratic society look like?" Liz asks. "I like when they talked about idleness," says Dylan. "Instead of being violent, he just wants to see movement away from a standstill culture and it's the responsibility of everyone who sees things that they don't feel are right—and that things that may look like they're normal can be wrong." "Do you feel it at all?" Liz asks as she takes her seat in the circle. Dylan uses the example of racism as a status quo that should be changed. "I think here at Kent we try to challenge the status quo, especially in our Community Action group—we start by looking at facts and figures and then moving into how to change things. But in the outside world, that's not as prevalent," says Paige. "How come?" asks Liz. "We're kind of a conformist society—the prospect that change will be unsuccessful. We don't want to take that risk at all for fear of having a negative effect on society. Like for the upper class, you don't want the society to change because maybe you'll lose some of the money you've accumulated over the years," says one student. "The tax structure, the health-care bill—a lot of people are worried that the government is going to take property from us to solve the problems." Melanie speaks up, "Someone has to stir the pot. Even though I feel like at Kent it's drilled into us, it's a good thing—like, my other friends outside of Kent will say things that are socially accepted by the status quo, but I speak up. At first they're just, like, 'Whatever', but then they stop." "What's that like with friends who haven't been exposed to these ideas? Are they our stand-ins for the rest of America? Sounds like you've been brave enough to broach it with them," says Liz. "It's easier because I've known them for a while and then they shy away from what they just said," Melanie responds. "A lot of kids these days—typical teenagers in TV shows want to fit in and go with the flow, we don't see that much at Kent. We are different in a good way—we try to make a difference all the time. They don't pay attention to that stuff," says a student. Another says, "I think the question isn't *will* we change but *can* we? The political disparity between Democrat and Republican—everything is split two sides which just makes it impossible to really accomplish much." Liz says, "The reading in PHS today dealt with that—the Dixiecrats had hijacked the Democratic Party. It's not about the will to change, but the ability. We just saw what happened to pass a health-care bill. To watch legislation get made—it took such an effort and the result is we got a bill with some change, but maybe not as much as we could." Another student says, "It's almost naïve—the PHS authors didn't know. Naïve in a good way because they were clean, not tarnished by the past which kind of let them go pursue their goals freely." "So they were able to have a new vision because they were unattached to these old things?" restates Liz. "And as a student you have less commitments than an adult—you're able to freely change your mind because you're not worried about paying your bills," says Paige. "That's why people rely on students so much," says Andy. "Adults have a role in society to maintain a lifestyle and as kids we're going to be leading a future without them so they want us to direct the future of change and doing something with our lives and reform." "Do you see this generation as reformers? Are we on the uptick?" asks Liz. "It's definitely in front of us," one student replies. "Regarding my initial thought, the whole idea with us doing more reform within society has changed from what our idea of reform was two generations ago. Then it was worrying about foreign threats and what our stance was and now that we're an established super power, we can look towards reforming our own flaws within our own society and we can look towards homelessness, the drug war, etc." "And yet we're still in two foreign wars that are draining our treasury," counters Liz. Dylan says, "I actually disagree—we *are* a superpower, but we're still preoccupied with foreign policy. There's more talk about Iraq than there is about homelessness. I'm in the homelessness group and no one's doing anything—people aren't doing enough." "So there's more consciousness, but actual action? You see more flaws," says Liz. Adam bickers with her about wanting to disagree with him. "I want to be a child of the 60s," says Dylan. "Like that woman came to speak to us about the modern Freedom School. She was talking about how our generation knows so much but has no movement so we should go be angry about it. We don't get angry about the injustices we see. No one is struck enough by the things that we're living right now." Finally Jennifer is called on. "I definitely see it—the suburb I used to live in is really White, WASPy, and conservative. When I go out there, they don't even know the PHS exists. Sometime it annoys me because they say, "That's so gay" or "fag" or something that's a little bit racist and that's when I start calling them out and they say it's not a big deal." "So most kids haven't had this kind of education," says Liz. "Our sectional soccer game had not a single Black person," adds Dylan. "And I bet that's why your parents are here—they want you guys to be exposed. They presumably could have moved to a suburb, they could have chosen a homogeneous sheltered life," says Liz. "Do you think the youth today aren't organized?" asks Rachel of Dylan. "We're not disorganized or stupid," says Dylan. "You have the greatest tool for connection ever—the Internet and Facebook, despite all its ills," says Liz. Justin says, "I'm hopeful, though. When we're those old geezers—" "You'll be more enlightened old geezers?" teases Liz. "Just because we're conscious about problems of our society shows that we're on the uptick—the next step we need to do is to take action. The 1960s generation has been romanticized like Forrest Gump. I've been downtown for a gay-rights march and the environmental movement—kids in almost every school are taking action. We're just starting to find what our passions are but we *are* finding them," says Paige. Rachel says, "I think we can be considered a reincarnation of the youth of the 1960s, but it's just more normal now to be protesting, to be marching whereas some of the things we've romanticized." "Let me ask you this. What makes you angry about your inheritance?" says Liz. She quotes Hayden. "Their inheritance was Jim Crow, nuclear weapons, the lingering effects of McCarthyism, the Cold War—they're angry about it because they didn't create any of that stuff. We have to participate in society to bring down these horrible things. From the point of view of your action group, what makes you angry?" Paige said, "The one thing I'm really upset about that I just sort of realized this year was the disparity between schools." "I am angry about that, too. How unfair it is that kids exactly like you—no difference in intelligence—other than the fact that they live in a neighborhood where they're going to go to a crappy school and it's just going to perpetuate," Liz agrees. Adam says, "That social cycle of perpetuating." Liz explains how there are no sophomore sports in the city's public schools. Justin hasn't heard about this and looks shocked. "They're cutting arts programs—these disparities are getting worse." Rachel adds, "I was going to say the same thing. It's such a natural thing—you grow up, you go to school. Education has always been around, it's something that should be the easiest fix, it provides jobs, it helps our economy by making kids smarter. You would think it would be a huge priority." Melanie says, "Mine is more just the outlook of people—they're just so pessimistic. I know there's a part where you have to speak realistically. In the PHS they talked about listlessness, when they could do something—even if it's not that much, yet people are just, like, sitting." Jane says, "It makes me think of gay rights and I think it's kind of weird—we fought for African American civil rights and now we've inherited a new outcast group and I think it's kind of sad. They're normal people and they want to lead normal lives and previous generations have been ignorant of that." She cites anti-gay activist Fred Phelps specifically. "He believes they're the spawn of the devil and it's sad that no one thinks they should have rights." Liz continues around the circle. One student talks about the city's funding for homelessness and how the majority of it goes to projects that are used for tourism. "So, the issue is misallocation of resources and lack of commitment to things that really ought to be priorities?" restates Liz. Another student says, "We can't be naïve like them—I want to be naïve like them but due to the status quo, in order to be successful, you have to be knowledgeable so we can't start with a clean slate." Liz asks him to rephrase what makes him angry. "That we're stuck with what it's in the past and we can't start clean," he says. Another says, "Mine relates to my group—on a daily basis, literally, we automatically tie inferiority to race. But you can use that to anything—my group is religious pluralism and we talk about Arab Americans and Muslims." "So the lingering hierarchy?" asks Liz. "Yeah—seriously. Someone's not automatically a terrorist," he says. Dylan adds her thoughts: "I would have to agree with Paige—a really poorly-run city school is just depressing, the manner in which the teachers just like speak to the kids. I can't see how you can expect someone to come out of there and not be emotionally destroyed. The public school system here is like a factory, which gets people through so they can get away with saying that they've done their job. Everything starts there which makes me angry that it's been so de-prioritized. If you want a prosperous, smart society of people, why wouldn't you teach them all that you know?" Andy says, "I'm sorry to keep bringing this up but I care about it which is why I'm in the group—one of the main problems I have isn't with homelessness but is with society. For our interviews, we interviewed the director of the Upper East Community Shelter and she said that people are so ignorant of homelessness and don't care about it. Obviously you pass by people every day but some people just don't care about providing for the homeless." "It's like the haves saying they don't want anybody near this. Someone else was bringing up, like, what does an illegal immigrant look like? What does a homeless person look like?" asks Liz. "Thirteen years of age is the average," says Dylan. "We need to make these issues our first priority—we have to step outside of our comfort zone and not violently fight for these causes, but show that we really care and not worry about being popular," says Jane. "Along the lines of inheritance, we're the rise of change—we're the generations in between and our grandkids will be the peak of that change." Dylan continues, "I was just thinking about party politics and right now we're very divided and those two are reaching farther apart every day. When I was reading the PHS I noticed how universally it all seemed like a good idea regardless of what you are. Participating in what you want to be—that transcends party lines. That's what it's going to take—an issue that lets us see that, but something has to happen where we become one force instead of the Republican youth or the Democratic youth." "I disagree with that," says Jennifer. "I thought there were lots of jabs at conservatism—I pulled a quote and wrote about it in my homework. I think it is divided right now, but personally—I don't know how to put this without getting yelled at. I think a lot of change has to happen, but we've *been* changing. We change at a slower pace because we have to. The US is a superpower and now we're coming to a slower pace and are changing with the nations around us and I think that's the right track instead of all this reform *now* and *now* and *now* because otherwise it just overwhelms people sometimes. I've seen that with the Arizona law—securing our borders. People were yelling at me and telling me it supports racial profiling. But we have to secure our borders." "But 'Don't Ask, Don't Tell'? That's a party politics thing," says Dylan. "I'm not for that," says Jennifer. Rachel says, "Even within the Democratic Party there is a division—so the parties are divided but against each other, too." Liz looks at the clock and realizes it is time for class to end. She says, "I think you're on to something that change is incremental. One tiny step—maybe that's the best we can hope for? Fascinating discussion, you guys." Afterwards, I asked Liz about the direction the conversation took. "I finally asked the right question," she tells me. She had thought she wanted them to articulate a vision about what they are going to do as adults in relation to the PHS, but had begun to realize that they are distracted with impending finals and upcoming applications to colleges. "So maybe it's more about focusing on questions of what makes them angry." I ask her what value she thinks the action groups have. "I do feel like the program has opened their eyes, but this is the moment when we try to get them to make some sort of commitment, but maybe that's the wrong way to look at it. What blocks participatory democracy? What did you inherit? What stands in the way of you getting involved?"

Like Vernon's vignette, this transcript of Liz's class at Kent Academy is ripe for multiple analyses: how Liz positions the students as special, how students educated their entire lives at private school conceptualize public schools, how they construct the suburbs as homogeneous despite their own homogeneity, etc. What I want to focus on, however, is the skillful way in which Liz managed to help her students interpret an important historical document (the "Port Huron Statement") that has direct connections to their lives as privileged youth and as members of social action groups. In terms of content, an Educating Activist Ally model demands that teachers expose students to multiple perspectives, explicitly connect facts and figures of social justice issues to students' daily lives, engage students' emotions and intellects, and contextualize injustices within individual acts and structural forces that reproduce injustice. Though there was only some attention to their emotions, Liz did explicitly engage students' ideas about social responsibility and their obligations to society by raising profound questions and listening to their answers. She sought out multiple perspectives for students to read and encouraged students to disagree with her and each other. The discussion was animated and engaged multiple students without much prompting from their teacher. Despite its problematic elements, this is a rich example of what kind of discussion can happen in just one class period attempting to introduce many of these difficult concepts.

What to Do on Monday

These vignettes and other examples from the two case studies are but brief demonstrations of the potential efficacy of this framework. By building upon the common characteristics of activities that elicited the intended responses of social justice pedagogy among privileged students in Liz and Vernon's classrooms (two very different contexts of privilege), it holds great promise as a framework to help teachers plan and reflect on their curricular and pedagogic decisions. Of course, it is wise to remember that no one model guarantees that privileged students will take up a particular identity, Activist Ally or otherwise. Any teacher knows that a singular proposal for curing all that ails schools is as believable as advertisements for old-fashioned snake oil. While an Educating Activist Allies framework does not (nor cannot) fully remedy tensions within social justice pedagogy for privileged students, it does highlight their unique experiences and challenges them to reject the tempting embrace of weak social obligations and a thin theory of justice that protects their privilege and reproduces the status quo.

I am going to shift my authorial voice here a bit and talk directly to those teachers and teacher educators interested in implementing this model so as to be as clear as possible. I propose a few basic steps to help you begin (though "basic" here is misleading—anyone who cares about their teaching knows well how many hours, days, and months that creating curriculum can consume). First, solicit your students' ideas about privilege, injustice, and the relationship between the two (e.g., one-on-one conversations, class discussions, written essays, and art projects). The questions at the end of Chapter 5 are particularly helpful here: what power do we have? When and where do we have it? Why do we have that power? What do we do with that power? In what ways should that power be more justly distributed?[2] I cannot stress enough the importance of genuinely listening to your students in order to understand them rather than listening only to correct or reprimand them. In and of themselves, such conversations are an example of the Educating Activist Allies model in action, and help to establish a baseline of sorts to determine how your students are thinking about these issues.

Next, analyze their responses for areas of growth by using the modes of thinking described in Chapter 5. Are students struggling with understanding the structural forces at play in systemic injustice? Are they dismissive of marginalized voices and stories? Are they unwilling or unable to identify examples of injustice in their midst? In addition, consider the insights from Chapters 3 and 4 here. In what ways is your context of privilege unique? Ought you be engaged in bursting the bubble or disturbing the comfortable? What does that mean for your practice? What expectations from students, parents, and administrators may be constraining you? How might you negotiate these tensions and obstacles?

After better understanding the context of your teaching, develop learning activities that align with the criteria of the model. Keep in mind that these criteria were developed as I sorted activities for those that encouraged an Activist Ally response and those that encouraged Meritocrat, Benevolent Benefactor, and Resigned responses. Those that emphasized intellectual and emotional personal connections to injustice, required critical self-reflection, prioritized listening to each other as well as marginalized voices, and offered opportunities to build relationships with people from backgrounds different than them over time tended to produce more of the desired responses among privileged youth (awareness, agency, and action). For some teachers, this may require only slight adjustments in course readings or final-project descriptions. Vernon, for instance, was excited to plan more opportunities for formal reflection in association with the field trips and to brainstorm with the other teacher in the school exchange to develop a collaborative unit among their students. For others, it may mean rethinking the way their course is structured. Liz, for example, had redesigned her course so that her students studied the same chronology of history four times through different lenses with rich social justice potential rather than as one giant narrative march from Reconstruction to whenever she could rush by the end of the semester. Do not feel pressured to overhaul your entire curriculum at the outset. Based on what your students have communicated to you and what you know about your community (and what you know about your own abilities), target those areas that are most in need of your professional attention.

Lastly, engage in continuous critical reflection on your practice. Ask a critical friend or colleague to review your course materials and unit plans. Are they meeting the criteria of the model? Have you explicitly connected students' lives and communities to the circumstances of injustice, questioned who is routinely positioned as experts, and widened the range of people with whom the students have opportunities to build relationships? In what ways can these elements be deepened and strengthened? In addition, have someone observe your class. How might weak conceptions of justice be reinforced by classroom dynamics? Are multiple perspectives encouraged or stifled in your class? Importantly, ground your reflection in continued conversation with your students about these issues. Document their growth. And have patience. I am a firm believer that we never know what students are going to do with these lessons years from now.

There is no doubt that this is challenging work that faces many obstacles and challenges. Like Vernon and Liz, there will be times when you may fall short of your vision for good teaching or your students may say and do things you find abhorrent. You may yourself say or do something regretful, injurious, or wrong. However, like Vernon and Liz, there will also be times when you facilitate learning opportunities that help students see with new eyes and inspire them to engage with the world as "Activist Allies." For those committed to social justice pedagogy, these are the moments that sustain and guide us; I hope you have many.

APPENDIX A

The positioning of myself as a multicultural subject in a sociopolitical contextual would be important at the outset of any study, but is made particularly so in a qualitative, critical investigation of how privilege functions in education by someone who identifies herself as privileged. Though I recognize that it cannot entirely extricate me from being too close to the issues I study, naming myself as someone who struggles every day to question and critique the systems that in many ways privilege me is one small contribution I can make to "defect" from the silence surrounding such systems and to interrupt the hegemonic forces of oppression at work (e.g., McIntosh, 1990; Johnson, 2006; Wise, 2008).

An Insider's Perspective

I am the eldest of two daughters born to a middle-class, White family living in an almost exclusively (and exclusive) White suburb of Des Moines, Iowa. My mother ran a small piano-lesson studio from the basement of our small ranch home while my father worked as a news anchorman for the local CBS affiliate, a job that afforded more local celebrity than income. Though my sister and I grew up without wanting for material comforts and necessities, we knew that the priority of our parents' budget was quality time as a family rather than material goods. Despite this modesty, we had access to the lifestyle of suburban excess through our friends and classmates of the "new middle class" (Apple, 2006). Much like West Town depicted in this study, my experiences at school match Anyon's (1980) description of *affluent professional schools* where children acquire symbolic capital with the intention it be applied for future social power and financial reward. We were "concertedly cultivated" (Lareau, 2003), taught to set ourselves apart from (or above) others in order to maintain, if not increase, the privilege we had.

The "we" in this sentence is not inclusive of all the students at the school given that we were a heavily tracked bunch. As someone who excelled at standardized tests and met teachers' expectations of "good" behavior, I was placed in AP sections of courses with few opportunities for classroom interactions with kids of color or low-income students and, subsequently, socialized in similarly segregated circles. The only people of color in my life were children of professional-class South Asian immigrants or children who White families had adopted. While I do not remember hearing any explicitly racist comments while growing up, neither did I hear any explicitly *racial* comments (Pollock, 2004). Adults in the community typically adopted the (not atypical) White attitude that it was neither necessary nor polite to discuss race (or class, for that matter) (Berlak & Moyenda, 2001; Landsman, 2001; Leonardo, 2009).

After graduation, most of my friends left high school for elite colleges while I accepted a scholarship to a small state university that was more affordable for my family and kept me close for visits home. The campus was starkly homogeneous and attracted mostly conservative, White, working-class students from nearby small towns. I majored in teaching, primarily because of the reputation of the School of Education. Though I did not notice its absence at the time, there was little attention to multiculturalism, social justice, or critical theory in my teacher-education classes. The history department, however, turned me on to writers like Howard Zinn and Ronald Takaki and emphasized the importance of engaging multiple perspectives. My time at the Catholic student center also supported these ideas in conversations about injustice with a fiery nun. In addition, my scholarship afforded me access to seminars encouraging social critique and study-abroad opportunities in Spain and Russia that exposed me to different parts of the world. By the time I returned home to student teach, my worldview had been irreversibly expanded; my hometown seemed familiar and comfortable yet frustratingly uncritical and seemingly unaware of a world outside.

My first job out of college was a high-school social studies position in a rural working-class community in southeastern Minnesota. Racially and ethnically, the community mirrored my hometown, though such homogeneity stuck out to me as never before: there were as many stoplights as Black students (i.e., one) and only a handful of Laotian immigrants' children and recently emigrated Mexicans whose parents worked at the local meat-packing plant. The traditions and customs of a small working-class community, however, were completely new to me. The district's schools, in many ways, fit Anyon's (1980) descriptions of *working-class* and *middle-class schools* preparing students for mechanical, routine work.

In complete contrast with this world, I spent my summers working at a boarding school, a perfect example of Anyon's (1980) *executive elite* school preparing students for intellectual work and cultivating symbolic capital. My students included the children of the world's wealthiest families as well as "scholarship kids" from low-income families in Memphis, TN and students from the Navajo Nation. I deeply enjoyed teaching in such culturally diverse classrooms and marveled at the school's wealth of resources, but grew frustrated that it enjoyed an international reputation of excellence despite having teachers that were no better or worse than my colleagues back home. I also recognized the ways in which my suburban upbringing had privileged me, but was shocked to enter into a world of the extreme elite—a world in which I knew I would never really belong.

These two jobs, dearly beloved, produced a continuous cognitive dissonance generating questions about the role of education in race and class privilege. In the fall of 2005, I left teaching with a desire to escape asinine interpretations of stipulations within the recently enacted No Child Left Behind Act and entered graduate school. I kept returning to the "problem" of how a social justice education informed by critical traditions and connected with progressive social movements can and should engage privileged people. These questions eventually evolved into my dissertation, which later evolved into this book.

Though any biography can only ever be a partial admission whose effects on its subject can ever be partially known, it hopefully assists the reader in making judgments about what lenses I may bring to my work. And though my complicity with these communities as a person privileged by race and class no doubt constrained aspects of my data collection, I am ultimately convinced that, in most instances, my background benefited this study in that I was able to use my experiences as an "insider" in the world of privileged schooling as a rapport-building strategy with participants.[1] The establishment of trust between myself and my participants built upon our shared backgrounds was not to manipulate them as fodder for an exposé, but rather to intuit what questions to ask, how to ask them, and how best to interpret the responses.

APPENDIX B

Epistemological Perspective

One's epistemological perspective is an important place to begin any discussion of research (Crotty, 1998). The greatest distinction among different epistemological camps lies between those adopting what can be classified as an empiricist/ objectivist/positivist stance and those who prefer an interpretivist/constructionist philosophy. In general, empiricists claim that knowledge is legitimately and conclusively derived from the sensory experience of an autonomous, detached subject. What unites interpretivists who challenge this stance is the belief that objective reality, constructed in and out of ever-changing human interactions and transmitted within multidimensional social contexts, can never be fully captured; that a thing can only be "known" through its interpreted representations (Crotty, 1998; Merriam, 1998; Denzin & Lincoln, 2003; Kincheloe & Tobin, 2006; Gerring, 2007). This challenges traditional notions of truth, but maintains space for some interpretations to be considered more liberatory, more accurate, and more useful than others (Stake, 1995; Crotty, 1998).

Although these understandings of the world are socially and historically constructed, they are nonetheless real in that they influence social actions and material existence (Apple, 1996). Building upon interpretivist understandings of the world, another epistemological approach pays special attention to issues of power, privilege, and oppression (Merriam, 1998). This stance pushes beyond interpretivism towards what Kincheloe (2005) calls *critical constructivism*. These criticalists "find contemporary society to be unfair, unequal, and both subtly and overtly oppressive for many people. We do not like it, and we want to change it" (Carspecken, 1996, p. 7). This is not to say that criticalist researchers only investigate certain topics or that their findings are predetermined to match what they hope to find. That would, quite simply, be bad research. Such "orientations" do have a lot to do with the choices one must make when beginning a research project: what to study and to what end. They also determine how findings will be used—what to publish and what to leave out, who to share the knowledge with and in what way (Carspecken, 1996). "Criticalist" research is, therefore, interpretivist inquiry into the socially constructed nature of power structures, culture, and human agency. My research investigating how privilege functions in social justice pedagogy in privileged communities is grounded in just such an epistemology.

Theoretical Frameworks

Though some would recommend an approach by which a researcher enters into an inquiry project with no stated a priori theoretical expectations, I contend that this is disingenuous (Stake, 1995; Brantlinger, 2003), not particularly useful (Nespor, 2006), and, ultimately, impossible. For this study, I ground my sense-making in the traditions of *critical theory* and *cultural historical activity theory*.

Critical Theory

Because I am concerned with how social class and racial privilege function within education and the ways in which a justice-oriented approach to teaching might shape how students privileged by unjust systems make sense of their responsibilities, it makes sense that I would be inspired by critical theory. There is no one "correct" definition of critical theory, but rather a tradition inspired by the Marxist social analyses of the Frankfurt School and furthered by critical scholars from Europe and the United States whose educational research was published in the 1970s and 1980s (e.g., Althusser, 1971; Apple, 1971, 1979; Bernstein, 1975; Bourdieu & Passeron, 1977; Anyon, 1980; Willis, 1981; Apple & Weis, 1983; Bourdieu, 1984; Whitty, 1985). This work gathered steam with critiques of Bowles & Gintis' (1977) class-based analysis of schooling and expanded in the 1980s and 1990s to power-fully complicate understandings of sociocultural and economic reproduction by considering the ways in which class interacts with race and gender. In recent years, feminist, queer, and critical race scholars (e.g., Kumashiro, 2002; Gillborn, 2008; Leonardo, 2009) as well as those influenced by Foucauldian-inspired conceptions of power (e.g., Youdell, 2006) continue to push the boundaries of the critical tradition in education.

A critical theoretical framework thus challenges the belief systems and social relations that (re)produce power differentials (Apple, 1996), promotes inquiry that fosters enlightened self-knowledge and social action (what Freire (2000) called *conscientização*), and encourages self-reflection (Brantlinger, 2003). Attention to power relations and the reproduction/interruption of social inequalities are embedded in this study's data collection and analysis. It is also woven into my core assumptions about schooling, most notably the belief that schools can and should be sites for the cultivation of a collective sensibility that is grounded in a conception of human flourishing and directly challenges the individualism and competitiveness at the heart of a neoliberal ideology permeating American society today.

Cultural Historical Activity Theory

My research is also grounded in cultural historical activity theory (CHAT), a relatively under-used framework that can powerfully complement and deepen critical theory (Roth & Lee, 2007).[1] This theoretical lens originated with the early-twentieth-century work of Russian psychologist Lev Vygotsky (1978), who critiqued the conventional psychological separation of the individual mind and its social context.[2] In CHAT research, the unit of analysis is a collective, artifact-mediated, and object-oriented social practice, or *activity*, seen in relation to other activity systems and thought of as historical and multi-voiced (Penuel & Wertsch, 1995). During formal inquiry grounded in CHAT, particular attention is paid to contradictions that emerge through this process of mediation. When subjects become conscious of them, these contradictions become the primary impetus for change and learning (Roth & Lee, 2007). These moments of "cognitive dissonance" are what Vygotsky (1978) called *zones of proximal development*. Though they are unpredictable and ephemeral, it is possible for teachers to try to create conditions and scaffold activities likely to facilitate such zones. These are the moments that sophisticate students' understandings of the world by pushing them into unfamiliar or even uncomfortable intellectual territory (Engeström, 2009). In a broad sense, social justice pedagogy can be conceived as just such a strategy.

By applying Engeström's (2009) conception of "critical conflicts" and "double binds," I thought about data documenting a student's resistance to the pedagogy not as a negative characteristic or something "gone wrong," but rather as a student's visible movement through a zone of proximal development and/or their exercise of agency with regard to the activity's object (Roth & Lee, 2007). Operating under a CHAT framework also helped me to see classroom elements as mutually constitutive and in flux. That fluidity is not entirely unpredictable or without pattern, however; just as a river maintains a familiar course while still constantly in motion, CHAT is mindful that there are sets of *rules* governing socially-mediated space that constrain and shape the possibilities for how that space is mediated.

Critical Theory and CHAT

One of the most influential of these constraints is the sociopolitical and economic contexts of intensifying forms of globalized, neoliberal capitalism that use schooling to encourage competitive individualism, privilege privatization, and reify a market systems ideology (Apple, 2006; Weis, Fine, & Dimitriadis, 2009). Quite simply, our society is raced, classed, gendered, etc. in ways that privilege Whiteness, encourage meritocratic myths of social-class mobility, normalize growing wealth inequality, and support patriarchal norms.[3] These "rules" deeply influence what is likely to happen in our world. In this study, economic and social conditions helped shape the populations of participating students in this study who have been segregated and privileged by race and social class. That there even exist "suburban" communities and private schools sheltered within elite enclaves of the city, or that a tradition such as "social justice pedagogy" has any meaning at all—none of this is happenstance; these realities are all products of socioeconomic and political phenomena we can document with ample historical evidence. To divorce an analysis of students' learning (especially learning about injustice) from this context would be absurd and reckless.

When CHAT is explicitly connected with critical theory, the ways in which power functions in an activity come into sharper focus. The work of Howard (2008) is valuable not only because he is one of the few scholars explicitly linking these two theoretical traditions, but also because he is specifically concerned with the role of privileged identities in students' mediation of pedagogy. His understanding of these two theoretical frameworks in relation to each other ("ideologically mediated action") is worth quoting at length:

> Cultural meanings, or ideologies ... are neither imposed, hegemonic structures nor stable. Individuals do not perform pre-scripted parts in enacting and practicing their identities. These identities are being constantly shaped and reshaped by the complex interactions of individuals' everyday realities and lived experiences. ... This more critical approach to understanding identity as ideologically mediated action provides a framework useful in articulating an alternative conceptualization of privilege to that which has dominated much of the literature on privilege for the past two decades or so. This critical framework can be used to shift the focus from identifying *what* privilege is to exploring *how* privilege is produced and reproduced. By examining how privilege is actively produced and reproduced, we draw attention to the salience of privilege for understanding the workings of everyday life and for fashioning particular ways of knowing and doing. ... This critical approach allows us to elaborate and extend our understanding of the available cultural processes and meanings individuals use to construct a privileged identity. ... By mapping out and exposing the contours of privilege, we can begin to imagine the possibilities for interrupting the processes that reinforce and regenerate privilege.
>
> *(p. 31)*

Though he is focused on identity formation rather than on modes of thinking, the emphasis in my project, I aim to extend the work of Howard (2008) by looking at these "contours of privilege" within a social justice classroom whose object is challenging the reproduction of oppressive power relations inherent in racist, capitalist systems.

Methodology

With my research questions defined and my epistemological and theoretical frameworks articulated, I now turn to describe the methodology and data collection methods used in my formal inquiry. In particular, it is helpful to clarify the terms I use given that research terminology is frequently inconsistent and contradictory. First, I distinguish between ethnography and case study (and their "critical" counterparts); next I justify the use of a comparative critical ethnographic case-study research design for this project; and lastly I lay out the specific tools used to explore my research questions.

Occasionally, "ethnography" is used interchangeably with "case study" (Merriam, 1998). Ethnography as a methodology was born out of an anthropological tradition focused on observing, recording, and analyzing culture in its complexity and everyday setting (Crotty, 1998). According to Anderson-Levitt (2006), ethnography is less a methodology and more of a "research philosophy" that is best applied when researchers are "not exactly sure what the problem is" (p. 282). Most ethnographers recommend following Geertz's (1977) advice to produce a "thick description" of the structures of meaning and symbols that make up its conceptual world for the richest possible understanding of a culture. Case studies can be "ethnographic" if they are focused on a thick description of lived cultural practices, though they may also be historical, more focused on one aspect of a culture, or quantitative in nature (Yin, 2003).

In contrast with an ethnography, which looks at a cultural group across sites, a case study, however, is a descriptive, interpretive, or evaluative analysis of a single unit or bounded system—a "case" (Merriam, 1998).[4] Scholars agree that a "case" is a unit of *lived activity* that can only be understood *in context* (Merriam, 1998; Gillham, 2000; Gerring, 2007). Stake (1995), one of the foremost scholars of case study, defines it as "the study of the particularity and complexity of a single case, coming to understand its activity within important circumstances" (p. xi). Because of its contextual nature, these circumstances or boundaries are, admittedly, not always easy to draw and will include "many more variables of interest than data points" (Yin, 2003, p. 13). The cases of this particular study were bound by the time and space of two daily, semester-long social-studies courses. Though I spent time getting to know the schools, communities, and participants outside of class to understand the cases' contexts, the vast majority of my data collection occurred within the 50-minute class periods or in interviews with study participants.

While it is advocated as an "up-and-coming" approach to inquiry that has recently come into its own (Gillham, 2000), scholars warn of inevitable attack from those who challenge case study's notions of validity, reliability, and generalizability based upon empiricist epistemological grounds. These critics suggest that case study is only useful as either a teaching tool or as a preliminary step before "real research" begins (Gerring, 2007).[5] Yin (2003) challenges these concerns while acknowledging that the lack of methodological codification only lends credence to these criticisms. He claims that case study is not at the bottom of a scientific caste system, but rather can be used for important exploratory, descriptive, and explanatory purposes.[6] He stresses the importance of making clear that the goal is not *statistical*, but *analytic* generalization that expands theories. In his justification of the contemporary relevance of the Chicago school of sociology, Abbott (1997) makes a similar point that social facts are always contextually bound. A random sample drawn across contexts tends to pull social facts from the spaces that give them meaning and, in effect, renders them meaningless. Thus, it is in the particular cases, and only such cases, that we can understand social facts. In keeping with my criticalist epistemological and theoretical roots, I claim that a "critical case study," like its cousin "critical ethnography," is one that pays close attention to unequal power relations within a particular case and hopes to contribute knowledge that will help build a more just society.

Yin (2006) claims the case-study method is best applied to descriptive or explanatory questions (What happened? How or why did something happen?), which are grounded in contemporary settings that make the relevant behaviors difficult to manipulate. My research queries are just such questions and the settings I chose, high-school social-studies classrooms attempting social justice pedagogy, are relevant and not something I sought to manipulate. The two cases I have chosen to study are "instrumental" (Stake, 1995) and "crucial" (Gerring, 2007) in the sense that I hope a greater understanding of social justice teaching with privileged students emerges from my research and contributes insights about this method of teaching and this group of students writ large. The decision to investigate two sites is based upon Yin's (2003) belief that multi-case designs offer analytic benefits and improve the chances of doing a good case study. This study is considered "cross-case" rather than comparative to respect the differences in each case's contexts. My intention is not to compare them, but to better understand each in relation to the other.

Data Collection and Analysis

Recruitment

Because radical educators in communities of privilege are anything but the norm, I used my best networking skills to find two self-described social justice educators willing to participate in a semester-long study. Several people, including one of my professors and a family friend, recommended Vernon Sloan. I met Liz Johnson through several serendipitous interactions with her colleagues in social justice pedagogy online chat rooms and from a recommendation from a professor. After visiting with both and getting site permission from the district and schools, we decided which semester-long classes I should observe daily based on logistical convenience and likelihood that students would participate. At suburban West Town High School, I committed to one section of Urban History, a social-studies elective open to juniors and seniors that examined historical and contemporary issues of West Town's parent city. The following semester, I sat in on two sections of U.S. History, a required course for juniors at Kent Academy in the city's Upper East neighborhood. Within the first week of each class, I recruited students to participate through a brief in-class presentation of my research questions, secured consent forms from the students and teachers, and began my data collection.

Challenges

Qualitative research and any study of human interactions is a decidedly messy and complex endeavor. In this study, this difficulty in documenting the complications of human experience was made more challenging by logistical constraints. Most notably, I was a single researcher able only to collect data from two classes for one semester apiece. Longitudinal data or comparative data of multiple-class sections within each site was simply not feasible. As I move forward, I hope to be able to increase the number of case studies for cross-case analysis and to touch base with students after several years in order to track their growth and development.

The study was also complicated by trying to gain access to communities like West Town and Upper East with a vested interest in avoiding problematization as a way to maintain their power (Anyon, 2006). Though most critical researchers maintain that unequal conditions are best seen from "below" (Apple, 1996), I propose that unequal conditions are best understood by including attention to what is happening "above." This is not to say that the voices of those benefiting from oppressive relations should be taken at face value or that their narratives should re-center them for the allocation of more resources (Angronsino & Mays de Perez, 2003, p. 110); rather, including them in critical analyses helps prevent them from becoming the unstated norm against which all other groups are compared. Is it only when the stories from above and below are brought to bear on each other that we can understand the full impact of our policies and practices (Khan, 2011).

In terms of conceptualizing the role of a researcher who looks up the social ladder, Brantlinger (2003) maintains that:

> The qualitative researcher's purpose clearly is not to give voice to the "traditionally silenced." Dominant voices, by definition, already are loud and influential. Furthermore, educated middle-class individuals are neither oppressed nor marginalized. They do not need researchers to advocate for them—they are extremely competent of self-advocacy. It may be unfair to

criticize the actions of generous participants or, especially, to deconstruct the narratives of the unsuspecting. Yet, the truth value of research with dominant people is more important than kindness and more likely to have an impact on equitable schooling than respect for participants.

(p. 28)

Though sympathetic to her aversion toward research that may unintentionally re-privilege the already privileged groups under study, I find her framing of critical analysis in this passage troublesome. Researchers of non-dominant groups are positioned as givers of voice and advocates of their participants; not only does such a role seem rooted in colonial forms positioning marginalized peoples as deficit ("giving voice" has a much more patronizing connotation than "secretarial work", for instance), but hopefully *all* analyses of the experiences of *any* population would involve deconstruction of narratives and constructive critique that is simultaneously respectful and critical. In this study, for example, while I witnessed many manifestations of privilege I have no desire to support, I also heard frustration and emptiness from the students that inspires me to advocate for better approaches to educating youth in these communities. Being critical and being an advocate are thus not mutually exclusive.

What is helpful in Brantlinger's work is the identification of a need to revisit ethical obligations of "studying up" with regards to the Human Subjects Review's requirements of respect, beneficence, and justice or Fontana & Frey's (2003) maxim "to our subjects first, to the study next, and to ourselves last" (p. 90). It is conceivable that a slightly different interpretation of research ethics is reasonable if the population under study is not marginalized (Tobin, 2006). For instance, ensuring avenues for recourse if exploited by the research may be less of a concern when working with a population that has access to ample means (both material and social) for redress. Even when studying populations much wealthier than myself, however, I must recognize that "the researcher is still in a privileged position, at least insofar as actually *doing* the research and disseminating its results are concerned" (Angrosino & Mays de Perez, 2003, p. 137). Additionally, the majority of my participants were youth who, however "privileged" they are still minors over which I have power simply by my status as an adult.

For this study, then, I followed Stake's (1995) advice for the collection of data no matter who the participants are:

> We seek to understand them. We would like to hear their stories. We may have reservations about some things the people … tell us, just as they will question some of the things we will tell about them. But we enter the scene with a sincere interest in learning how they function in their ordinary pursuits and milieus and with a willingness to put aside many presumptions while we learn.

(p. 1)

It is important to note that I came to genuinely care for the teachers and students in the study, many of whom I saw every day and with whom I spent significant time talking and listening. For the most part, these were funny, warm, welcoming, articulate, and interesting young people. Of course, I occasionally heard responses to my questions that troubled me or riled my own sense of right and wrong, but I appreciated that my role as a researcher pushed me to ask more questions and seek to understand their reasoning. I trust that my portrayal and analysis of these students and teachers are fair, humane, and honest. Member checks in which I have shared initial findings through email correspondence as well as conversations with the teachers and those students who were willing and able during and after the study to help me think through my findings convince me that I have done my best to balance compassion with critique.

Data-Collection Methods

To best understand what I observed and try to make sense of how the participants made sense of privilege and justice, I followed Yin's (2003) three principles of data collection: 1) using multiple, not just single, sources of evidence; 2) creating a case-study database (including case-study notes, documents, narratives); and 3) maintaining a chain of evidence. Because data collection is recursive and interactive in that analysis occurs simultaneously and often directs new means of collection, I regularly summarized my initial impressions and early conclusions which in turn generated new questions and led me to new sets of data (Merriam, 1998; Gillham, 2000; Yin, 2003). Though case study does not identify particular methods for collection or analysis, the most commonly cited options are observation, interviews, and document analysis (Merriam, 1998; Gillham, 2000).

Observations

Stake (1995) calls upon case-study researchers to be as "unobtrusive, as interesting, as wallpaper" (p. 59) though complete invisibility is, of course, impossible. In both classrooms, I acted as an observer-participant who the teachers acknowledged and welcomed into class activities and field trips. More often than not, I was treated as an extra set of hands to move desks, pass out papers, or look up information on my ever-present laptop during class discussions. All of the students and other teachers in the department knew me as Katy; even those not participating in the study chatted with me during breaks or in the halls. I always sat to the side or the back of the rooms, however, and sometimes entire class periods would go by without me saying nothing more than a quick greeting to students. Carspecken (1996) reminds us that "it is not the fact that the researcher's presence changes behaviors that is the problem, but rather that it is important to know *how behaviors have changed* if one's reconstructions are going to be penetrating" (p. 52). While it is impossible to know exactly how my presence changed behaviors, I discussed this with teachers and students who assured me that other sections or class periods for which I was not present were unfolding in similar ways.

My initial observations were informal notes jotted in a journal that helped me gain a general sense of activities and to build rapport with participants. As the semester continued, these observations became much more formal with detailed field notes (Stake, 1995; Tobin, 2006) taken on my laptop during class. Typically, I sat in on each section three or four days a week. I observed the physical setting, the participants' informal/formal interactions, the presentation of content, students' responses to the content including moments of cognitive dissonance, the legitimization of particular kinds of knowledge, and teachers' behaviors, as well as my own behavior (Merriam, 1998; Nespor, 2006). Though I tried to record utterances as precisely as I could, I also focused on participants' actions, tone of voice, and other non-verbal cues (Howard, 2008). My observational note-taking was "an ongoing project of configuring description and theory into larger patterns … [treating what I observed] as relationally constituted and foreground[ing] events, interactions, transactions, flows, and relations" (Nespor, 2006, p. 298).

Interviews

In addition to daily observations, I also conducted a series of semi-structured interviews with students and teachers, what Stake (1995) considers to be the "main road to multiple realities" in a case study. I modeled my interview style after what Joyce & Tutela (2006) call "conversation," a "feminine way of knowing" and a "dialectical act" that encourages a connection between the people talking rather than a detached, unidirectional approach that prevents interviewers from expressing feelings or answering questions. These conversations were not neutral tools of data gathering, but active interactions that led to negotiated, contextually based results (Fontana & Frey, 2003).

Though I conducted interviews with such an interactive style in mind, I still planned ahead with a list of issue-oriented questions that helped focus the conversations (Stake, 1995; Fontana & Frey, 2003; Yin, 2003). During initial interviews, participating students and teachers provided biographical information and self-identified themselves politically, racially, and economically. Subsequent interviews involved reflecting on critical incidents in class as well as explicitly discussing varying conceptions of justice and privilege. The interviews tended to last from between twenty minutes to an hour depending on how much time participants had. I recorded these conversations using Audacity software that an assistant later transcribed for analysis. Students and I met one-on-one three times throughout the semester while the teachers and I had informal conversations almost every day in addition to five formal interviews. Emails generated throughout the life of the study also served as conversational data.

Documents

In addition to observations and interviews, I collected piles of papers and books from both classrooms. In a case study, the most important uses of documents are to corroborate and augment evidence from another source and to make inferences that help guide further data collection (Yin, 2003). Throughout the study, I collected the two course syllabi, the course texts, class-assignment sheets, student work with teacher feedback, supplemental-course readings, other content materials (e.g., references for documentary films, posters, and primary-source documents), and school newspapers. I also collected student commentary about the classes available from online websites like "ratemyteacher.com" and online learning sites affiliated with the course.

Data analysis

As advised by the case-study methodological standards that exist, I concurrently collected data and analyzed it using themes generated by my initial research questions as well as themes that emerged on their own (Lincoln & Guba, 1985; Stake, 1995; Yin, 2006). This "circular process" involved a "movement from the tacit (intuitive and undifferentiated) toward the explicit (delineated and differentiated) and then back to the holistic" (Carspecken, 1996, p. 95). I conducted my analysis with the hope of finding patterns of some sort, identified through direct interpretation of an individual instance as well as through an aggregation of instances (Stake, 1995; Nespor, 2006). Such categories are particularly important with instrumental case studies (Stake, 1995) and should be exhaustive, mutually exclusive, sensitizing, and conceptually congruent (Merriam, 1998).

While in the process of data collection, I devised categories based on patterns that emerged from the data (both within and across data sets from both cases) as well as from the application of a priori themes related to my theoretical frames (Yin, 2003). I confirmed those categorical codes with critical friends and the participating teachers. I then coded all documents and transcripts by hand using Microsoft Word. For example, one of the emergent themes was how students thought about their communities. Within this theme, one of the coding categories was the word "bubble." I searched each transcript for the word "bubble," copied the quote using the Microsoft Word copy function, pasted it into a separate file specific to the code, then cited its source. Each code thus had its own file and each file was bundled together in a theme folder. Though I am well aware that sophisticated software exists to assist in this analysis, I found it easier to work with Word and believed it allowed me closer contact with the data. This was especially important to me as my analysis relied upon emergent categories for coding.

As my analysis grew more complex, I took time to share it with the teachers and interested students for feedback. According to Brantlinger (2003), critical researchers must "analyze the underlying, tacit meanings of narratives and [are] often highly critical of certain participants' thinking and actions" (p. 28). While these "tacit" meanings are certainly important, I maintain that we should not neglect the inclusion of participants' own understandings in research; an understanding of one depends on an understanding of the other. Subsequently, there are aspects of my analysis that came as a surprise to my participants during member-checks who would never have drawn such conclusions on their own. I should note, however, that my interpretation has been met with support, curiosity, and, ultimately, confirmation—even those analyses which explicitly critique the choices and actions of the participants.

In whatever categories emerge during interpretation, it is essential that case-study researchers explain how their findings can be considered valid and reliable. For criticalist and interpretivist research, it is impossible to absolutely validate a researcher's interpretation of observations (Stake, 1995; Carspecken, 1996). This does not preclude validity and reliability within such research, but rather changes their meanings. The question is not whether findings are "replicable," but whether the results are consistent with the data collected (Merriam, 1998). Data source, investigator, theory, and methodological triangulation collects data from a variety of sources in a variety of ways and then checks these findings with participants and colleagues for conclusions that are suggestive rather than conclusive (Stake, 1995; Casrpecken, 1996; Crotty, 1998; Merriam, 1998; Yin, 2003).

Throughout my analysis, I engaged in this type of triangulation by sharing my evolving analysis with the participating teachers, interested students, and critical friends. This book is a result of those combined efforts to make sense of the data we generated and collected. Though certainly I learned much about the messiness of qualitative research through this project and hope to continue collecting more data related to these questions in the future, I stand by the data collected and analyzed here as well as my suggestive conclusions.

NOTES

1 Why the Education of Privileged Children Matters

1 2010 US census data points to a growing number of people of color and people below the poverty level in suburban areas, municipalities that are ill-equipped to provide much-needed social services (Allard & Roth, 2010).

2 "Maleficiary" is a word I invented here to mean the opposite of "beneficiary" or one whose actions/intentions are thwarted rather than enabled.

3 In addition, there are powerful combinations of privilege that arise out of the intersections among these forms of privilege like those between race and class or class and gender (Grant & Sleeter, 1986; Wright, 1997).

4 Wright and Rogers (2010) also point out three other less tangible consequences of a highly competitive, individualistic capitalist society: the erosion of community; the commercialization of "morally-salient" aspects of life like child care, the arts, religion and spirituality, and the value of a human life; and the cultivation of skills and dispositions that favor exiting a situation rather than voicing dissatisfaction with it.

5 Perhaps more than any other recent work, Annette Lareau's (2003) classic book *Unequal Childhoods: Class, Race, and Family Life* provides vivid accounts of how parents negotiate such a system and what that means for children's experiences of schooling.

6 Though he does not focus as heavily on the reproduction of social class privilege, Apple (1982, 1995, 1996) has produced influential work in understanding class reproduction within educational policies and practices.

7 In an appendix table compiled by Bill Sparks, Derman-Sparks & Ramsey (2006) include other examples about the history of White resistance to racism in the United States (pp. 163–166). In his memoir, Tim Wise (2008) also includes examples of anti-racist Whites in American history.

2 Disconnected, Paralyzed, and Charitable

1 A quick but crucial note: throughout the book, I use the term social justice pedagogy rather than social justice education because of my emphasis on classroom teaching and learning. Certainly, the two are intimately connected, but there are important distinctions. Social justice education more broadly addresses the structures of schooling,

the policies influencing schools, and teachers' relationship to that larger sociopolitical context. Social-justice pedagogy, on the other hand, focuses on the practices and work of teachers within a classroom context.

2 I regret if any of these tensions are read as dichotomous; much of the work regarding these questions has been quite nuanced and rightly refuses to given into "either/or" constructions. In the case of increasing opportunities for marginalized students or promoting anti-oppression activism, it is certainly possible to develop curriculum that does both. Such work is not easy, however, and there are no doubt times when teachers may feel pulled to lean more one way than another.

3 For a critique of the national focus on the "achievement gap" and the recommendation to instead attend to our nation's historical, economic, sociopolitical, and moral *debt* to children from marginalized groups, see Ladson-Billings (2006).

4 The exact text from the platform reads: "Knowledge-Based Education – We oppose the teaching of Higher Order Thinking Skills (HOTS) (values clarification), critical thinking skills and similar programs that are simply a relabeling of Outcome-Based Education (OBE) (mastery learning) which focus on behavior modification and have the purpose of challenging the student's fixed beliefs and undermining parental authority (p. 12)."

5 For a more detailed history of "social justice" and its role in education from Platonic to modern times, see Boyles, et al. (2009). For historic connections between youth activism and education, see Leistyna (2009).

6 North (2006) warns against spending too much time determining the oppressor's intentions, arguing that such a focus deleteriously shifts the focus away from those who are oppressed: "Although individual agency merits significant attention in theories of social justice, its implicit privileging of intentionality denies the actions and behavior of individuals that inadvertently result in injustice and/or are performed unconsciously" (pp. 524–525).

3 Sheltered and Exceptional

1 For those interested in doing such work, I urge them to join a burgeoning network of scholars investigating the education of privileged students by contacting me at kswalwel@gmu.edu.

2 More about these philosophies and what they can look like in practice can be found in Chapter 4.

3 See Lipsitz (2002) for an excellent historical description of how sub/urban policies in housing and development quite literally paved the way for a "White suburban identity" that absorbed ethnic Whites from the city and isolated Black and Latino communities. See also Anyon (2005) and Lipman (2011) for more about how housing and economic policies shape what happens in schools.

4 Home values have fallen and unemployment rates have risen in the last two years, however, due to the recession. Nearly 8% of residents are now unemployed, including the parents of two students in my study. This mother and father, however, were well-educated White lawyers and have been buffered from the worst effects of the recession given their assets and savings reserves. Nevertheless, the students reported anxiety and a noticeable change in their family's lifestyle.

5 Fifteen percent of graduates go on to two-year colleges, 1% enter the military, and another 1% immediately enter the workforce. Disaggregated racial/ethnic and social class data of these students was not available.

6 In his review of the psychological research related to affluent suburbs, Luthar (2003) takes care to note the disproportionate pressures to "be perfect" for suburban women.

7 When single-family houses are disaggregated from this data that includes townhomes and condominiums, the average home value is much higher: $1.5 million.

8 Interestingly, many of these letters blamed the lack of students of color on the "high numbers" of wealthy Jewish students. This opened up a heated school debate in the paper and student government forums about the type of student Kent should be attracting and educating.

4 Social Justice Pedagogy in Action

1 Not all of it represented the political Left (a cardboard cutout of Newt Gingrich smiles from the corner, for example, and a "JEB!" bumper sticker is on, appropriately, the right side of his podium), but most of it would be recognizable as tinted blue. Some are funny: "Jon Stewart for President '08" while others more explicitly provocative: "Vote Republican: It's Easier Than Thinking." Many pertain to specific issues: "Keep your laws off my body," "Sexism is a social disease," "My Country Invaded Iraq and All I Got Was This Expensive Gas," etc. There are posters of Mark Twain, Malcolm X, Mother Teresa, Che Guevara, Eleanor Roosevelt, and civil-rights activists famous for their work in the city.

2 Lending weight to these discussions was the historical context provided by the concurrent history unit addressing Jim Crow laws and the ways in which racism has been legislated into the fabric of the United States. Several times, Liz pointed out these connections in class and raised questions with the students about the ways in which they see Jim Crow extended into the 21st century.

5 Did They Get It?

1 I want to cite the influence of two conceptual models in the development of these four modes of thinking. The first is Edwards' (2006) aspiring social justice ally identity development framework that includes the *Ally for Self-Interest*, the *Ally for Altruism*, and the *Ally for Social Justice*. The second is Westheimer and Kahne's (2004) classification of types of citizenship: the *personally responsible citizen*, the *participatory citizen*, and the *justice-oriented citizen*. Though both were helpful in my analysis, neither was sufficient to explain the differences among students' responses.

2 The closer a student's name is to the center of a quadrant, the more consistently they expressed that frame's point of view. The closer the student's name is to the dividing line between two quadrants, the more they expressed a mixed point of view between those two frames. The italicized names are students from West Town High, the non-italicized names are students from Kent Academy.

3 It is important to note that these students universally self-identified as privileged simply for their association with the schools they attended. According to Xavier, for example, "Living in West Town alone is a privilege."

4 A particularly useful reading to help guide teachers asking these questions with their students is Chapter 10 ("Thinking About Fairness and Inequality") in Wright and Rogers' (2010) *American Society: How It Really Works*. It is available in open access text format at http://www.ssc.wisc.edu/~wright/ContemporaryAmericanSociety/Chapter%2010%20–%20inequality%20&%20fairness%20–%20Norton%20August.pdf

6 Eyes Pried Open

1 Curry-Stevens (2007) identifies five domains necessary for the transformation of privileged students: *spiritual changes* in which a student moves from an individual orientation to an interdependent connection, *ideological changes* in which students understand power relations and the importance of collective action, *psychological*

changes that call for sensitive educators to facilitate reflective discussions that border on counseling, *behavioral changes* that come about with structured time for practicing social action, and *intellectual or cognitive changes* that form a new sense of social responsibility.
2 Clearly, these questions would be a powerful foundation for any social justice teacher working in any context, "privileged" or not.

Appendix A

1 I am reminded, however, of Gillham's (2000) advice that "even if you 'know' the setting you have to act as if you didn't: *because you don't*" (p. 18). I am also humbled by the many missteps I continue to make in my life as I learn to be an ally of people in marginalized communities.

Appendix B

1 Like critical theory, some researchers frame CHAT as an epistemology with implied methodologies. Scribner (1990) refers to it as a "metatheory." Frustrating to a novice researcher like myself is the lack of clarity with regards to what distinguishes epistemology, theoretical framework, and methodology.
2 In this "first generation" of CHAT, Vygostky (1978) laid out the foundations of his theory of mediated action. In the "second generation," Vygotsky's students Luria (1981) and Leont'ev (1978) critiqued his privileging of speech and incorporated into their explanations social, cultural, and historical dimensions from a Marxist perspective. This framework was introduced to American audiences by Michael Cole (1988) and expanded upon by Lave (1988, 1996), Rogoff (2003), Rogoff & Lave (1984), Scribner (1990), and Wertsch (1998) as well as the prolific Finnish scholar Engeström (1993, 1996, 1999, 2001) in a wave of "third-generation" research currently focusing on how activity systems interact with and influence each other. For a much more detailed history of CHAT and outlining of its tenets, see Roth & Lee (2007).
3 In his analysis of this "possessive investment of whiteness", Lipsitz (2002) provides a much thicker description than I have time to relay here of the layers of the historical economic and social policies and practices that have come to shape this reality.
4 The literature refers to "case study" as a method, methodology, and data collection tool. For this study, I refer to it as a methodology.
5 Barone (2006) posits that policymakers and politicians engage in such "blacklisting" to further a degenerative politics and defend against research that might remake the world for progressive ends.
6 Yin (2006) does advocate adhering to conventional "scientific" research design principles as defined by starting with explicit research questions, systematically collecting data, subjecting this data to a rigorous analysis, fairly presenting evidence, and relying on related literature to support claims.

REFERENCES

Abbott, A. (1997). Of time and space: The contemporary relevance of the Chicago school. *Social Forces*, 75(4), 1149–1182.

Adams, M., Bell, L.A., and Griffin, P. (Eds.) (1997). *Teaching for diversity and social justice: A sourcebook*. New York: Routledge.

Allard, S. & Roth, B. (2010). *Strained suburbs: The social service challenges of rising suburban poverty*. Washington, DC: Brookings Institution Metropolitan Policy Program.

Allegretto, S. (2011). The state of working America's wealth, 2011: Through volatility and turmoil, the gap widens. EPI Briefing Paper: State of Working America. Washington, DC: Economic Policy Institute.

Althusser, L. (1971). *Lenin and philosophy and other essays* (B. Brewster, Trans.). New York: Monthly Review Books.

Anderson-Levitt, K. (2006). Ethnography. In J.L. Green, G. Camilli, & P.B. Elmore (Eds.) *Handbook for complementary methods in education research* (pp. 279–296). Mahwah, NJ: Lawrence Erlbaum.

Angrosino, M.V. & Mays de Perez, K.A. (2003). Rethinking observation: From method to context. In N.K. Denzin & Y.S. Lincoln (Eds.) *Collecting and interpreting qualitative materials*. Thousand Oaks, CA: Sage Publications, 107–154.

Antrop-González, R. & De Jesús, A. (2006). Toward a theory of critical care in urban small school reform: Examining structures and pedagogies of caring in two Latino community based schools. *International Journal of Qualitative Studies in Education*, 19(4), 409–433.

Anyon, J. (1980). Social class and the hidden curriculum of work. *Journal of Education*, 162(1), 67–92.

Anyon, J. (2005). *Radical possibilities: Public policy, urban education, and a new social movement*. New York: Routledge.

Anyon, J. (2006). What counts as educational research? Notes towards a new Paradigm. In G., Ladson-Billings, (Ed.) *Research in the Public Interest* (pp. 17–26). New York: Teachers College Press.

Anyon, J. (2009). Critical pedagogy is not enough: Social justice education, political participation, and the politicization of students. In Apple, M., Au, W. & Gandin, L.A. (Eds.) *The Routledge international handbook of critical education* (pp. 389–395). New York: Routledge.

Apple, M. (1971). The hidden curriculum and the nature of conflict. *Interchange*, 2(4), 27–40.

Apple, M. (1979). *Ideology and curriculum.* New York: Routledge & Kegan Paul.

Apple, M. (1982). *Cultural and economic reproduction in education: Essays on class, ideology and the state.* London: Routledge & Kegan Paul.

Apple, M. (1993). *Official knowledge: Democratic education in a conservative age.* New York: Routledge.

Apple, M. (1995). *Education and power* (2nd ed.). New York: Routledge.

Apple, M. (1996). *Cultural politics and education.* New York: Teachers College Press.

Apple, M. (2006). *Educating the 'Right' way: Markets, standards, God, and inequality.* New York: Routledge.

Apple, M., Au, W., & Gandin, L.A. (Eds.) (2009). *The Routledge international handbook of critical education.* New York: Routledge.

Apple, M. & Beane, J. (2000). *Democratic schools: Lessons in powerful education* (2nd ed.). New York: Heinemann.

Apple, M.W. & Weis, L.M. (1983). Ideology and practice in schooling. In M.W. Apple & L.M. Weis (Eds.), *Ideology and practice in schooling* (pp. 3–33). Philadelphia, PA: Temple University Press.

Applebaum, B. (2007). White complicity and social justice education: Can one be culpable without being liable? *Educational Theory*, 57(4), 453–467.

Applebaum, B. (2009). Is teaching for social justice a "liberal bias"? *Teachers College Record*, 111(2), 376–408.

Applebaum, B. (2010). *Being White, being good: White complicity, White moral responsibility, and social justice pedagogy.* Lanham, MD: Lexington Books.

Aristotle. (1941). *The basic works of Aristotle.* R. McKeon (Ed.). New York: Random House.

Au, W. (2009). Fighting with the text: Conceptualizing and recontextualizing Freire's critical pedagogy. In M. Apple, W. Au, & L.A. Gandin (Eds.) *The Routledge international handbook of critical education* (pp. 221–231). New York: Routledge.

Au, W., Bigelow, B., & Karp, S. (2007). *Rethinking our classrooms: Teaching for equity and justice (Vol. 1).* Milwaukee, WI: Rethinking Schools.

Ayers, W., Hunt, J., & Quinn, T. (Eds.). (1998). *Teaching for social justice: A democracy and education reader.* New York: Routledge.

Ayers, W., Quinn, T., & Stovall, D. (Eds.). (2009). *Handbook of social justice education.* New York: Routledge.

Banks, J.A. (2004). Teaching for social justice, diversity, and citizenship in a global world. *The Educational Forum*, 64, 296–395.

Banks, J.A. & McGee Banks, C.A. (2006). *Multicultural education: Issues and perspectives.* New York: Wiley, John, & Sons.

Barone, T. (2006). Making educational history: Qualitative inquiry, artistry, and the public interest. In G. Ladson-Billings and W.F. Tate (Eds.) *Education research in the public interest: Social justice, action, and policy* (pp. 213–230). New York: Teachers College Press.

Barrett, J.R. & Roediger, D. (2002). How white people became white. In P.S. Rothenberg's (Ed.) *White privilege: Essential readings on the other side of racism* (pp. 29–34). New York: Worth Publishers.

Bell, L.A. (1997). Theoretical foundations for social justice education. In M. Adams, L. Bell, & P. Griffin (Eds.), *Teaching for diversity and social justice: A sourcebook* (pp. 3–15). New York: Routledge.

Berlak, A. and Moyenda, S. (2001). *Taking it personally: Racism in the classroom from kindergarten to college.* Philadelphia, PA: Temple University Press.

Bernstein, B. (1975). *Class, codes, and control, Volume 3* (2nd ed). London: Routledge.

Bernstein, J., McNichols, E., & Nicholas, A. (2008). *Pulling apart: A state-by-state analysis of income trends.* Washington, DC: Center on Budget & Policy Priorities.

Bickmore, K. (2008). Social justice and the social studies. In L.S. Levstik & C.A. Tyson (Eds.) *Handbook of research in social studies education* (pp. 155–171). New York: Routledge.

Bigelow, B., Harvey, B., Karp, S., & Miller, L. (Eds.) (2000). *Rethinking our classrooms: Teaching for equity and justice.* Milwaukee, WI: Rethinking Schools.

Bonnett, A. (1996). White studies: The problems and projects of a new research agenda. *Theory, Culture & Society,* 13(20), 145–155.

Bourdieu, P. (1984). *Distinction: A social critique of the judgment of taste* (R. Nice, Trans.). Cambridge, MA: Harvard University Press.

Bourdieu, P. & Passeron, J.C. (1977). *Reproduction in education, society, and culture.* London: Sage Publications.

Bowles, S. & Gintis, H. (1977). *Schooling in capitalist America: Educational reform and the contradictions of economic life.* New York: Basic Books.

Boyles, D., Carusi, T., & Attick, D. (2009). Historical and critical interpretations of social justice. In W. Ayers, T. Quinn, & D. Stovall (Eds.), *Handbook on social justice in education* (pp. 30–42). New York: Routledge.

Brantlinger, E. (2003). *Dividing classes: How the middle class negotiates and rationalizes school advantage.* New York: Routledge.

Buras, K. (2008). *Rightist multiculturalism: Core lessons on neoconservative school reform.* New York: Routledge.

Butin, D.W. (2002). This ain't talk therapy: Problematizing and extending anti-oppressive education. *Educational Researcher,* 31(3), 14–16.

Butin, D.W. (2007). Justice-learning: Service-learning as justice-oriented education. *Equity & Excellence in Education,* 40(2), 177–183.

Callan, E. (1997). *Creating citizens: Political education and liberal democracy.* New York: Clarendon Press.

Carspecken, P. (1996). *Critical ethnography in educational research.* New York: Routledge.

Centers for Disease Control and Prevention. (2011). Health disparities and inequalities report. *Morbidity & Mortality Weekly Report (MMWR) Supplement,* Volume 60, 1–116. Retrieved from www.cdc.gov/minorityhealth/CHDIReport.html#CHDIR.

Chaney, D. (1997). Authenticity and suburbia. In S. Westwood & I. Williams (Eds.) *Imagining cities: scripts, signs, memories* (pp. 137–147). London: Routledge.

Chizhik, E.W. & Chizhik, A.W. (2005). Are you privileged or oppressed? Students' conceptions of themselves and others. *Urban Education,* 40(2), 116–143.

Choules, K. (2007). The shifting sands of social justice discourse: From situating the problem with "Them," to situating it with "Us." *Review of Education/Pedagogy/Cultural Studies,* 29(5), 461–481.

Chubbuck, S. & Zembylas, M. (2008). The emotional ambivalence of socially just teaching: A case study of a novice urban schoolteacher. *American Educational Research Journal,* 45(2), 274–318.

Cochran-Smith, M. (2004). *Walking the road: Race, diversity, and social justice in teacher education.* New York: Teachers College Press.

Cole, M. (1988). Cross-cultural research in the socio-historical tradition. *Human Development,* 31, 147–157.

Conley, D. (2008). Reading between the lines (of this volume): A reflection on why we should stick to folk concepts of social class. In A. Lareau D. Conley (Eds.) *Social class: How does it work?* (pp. 366–374). New York: Russell Sage Foundation.

Cookson Jr., P.W. & Persell, C.H. (1985). *Preparing for power: America's elite boarding schools.* New York: Basic Books.

Crotty, M. (1998). *The foundations of social research: Meaning and perspective in the research process.* Thousand Oaks, CA: Sage Publications.

Curry-Stevens, A. (2007). New forms of transformative education: Pedagogy for the privileged. *Journal of Transformative Education,* 5(1), 33–58.

Darder, A., Torres, R., & Baltodano, M. (Eds.). (2002). *The critical pedagogy reader.* New York: Routledge.

Delpit, L. (1995). *Other people's children: Cultural conflict in the classroom.* New York: New Press.

Denis-McKay, Z. (2007). Seeing and being seen: Pedagogy for students of privilege. *Multicultural Review,* 16(3), 26–32.

Denzin, N.K. & Lincoln, Y.S. (Eds.) (2003). *Collecting and interpreting qualitative materials.* Thousand Oaks, CA: Sage Publications.

Derman-Sparks, L. & Ramsey, P.G. (2006). *What if all the kids are white? Anti-bias multicultural education with young children and families.* New York: Teachers College Press.

Dunne, J. (1993). *Back to the rough ground: "Phronesis" and "Techne" in modern philosophy and in Aristotle.* South Bend, IN: University of Notre Dame Press.

Dyer, R. (1988). White. *Screen,* 29, 45–62.

Edwards, K.E. (2006). Aspiring social justice ally identity development: A conceptual model. *NASPA Journal,* 43(4), 39–60.

Ellsworth, E. (1989). Why doesn't this feel empowering? Working through the repressive myths of critical pedagogy. *Harvard Educational Review,* 59(3), 297–324.

Engeström, Y. (1993). Developmental studies of work as a testbench of activity theory: The case of primary care medical practice. In S. Chaiklin & J. Lave (Eds.) *Understanding practice: Perspectives on activity and context* (pp. 64–103). Cambridge, UK: Cambridge University Press.

Engeström, Y. (1996). Interobjectivity, ideality, and dialectics. *Mind, Culture, and Activity,* 3, 259–265.

Engeström, Y. (1999). Activity theory and individual and social transformation. In Y. Engeström, R. Miettinen, & R.L. Punamäki (Eds.), *Perspectives on activity theory* (pp. 19–38). Cambridge, UK: Cambridge University Press.

Engeström, Y. (2001). Expansive learning at work: Toward an activity theoretical reconceptualization. *Journal of Education and Work,* 14(1), 133–156.

Engeström, Y. (2009). The future of activity theory: A rough draft. In A. Sannino, H. Daniels, & K. Gutierrez (Eds.) *Learning and expanding with activity theory.* New York: Cambridge University Press.

Erickson, G. (2009). Un/taming Freire's pedagogy of the oppressed. In M. Apple, W. Au, & L.A. Gandin (Eds.) *The Routledge International Handbook of Critical Education* (pp. 232–239). New York: Routledge.

Evans, A., Evans, R., & Kennedy, W. (1995). Pedagogies for the non-poor. Eugene, OR: Wipf and Stock.

Foley, N. (2002). Becoming Hispanic: Mexican Americans and whiteness. In P.S. Rothenberg's (Ed.) *White privilege: Essential readings on the other side of racism* (pp. 49–60). New York: Worth Publishers.

Fontana, A. & Frey, J.H. (2003). The interview: From structured questions to negotiated text. In N.K. Denzin & Y.S. Lincoln (Eds.) *Collecting and interpreting qualitative materials.* Thousand Oaks, CA: Sage Publications, 61–106.

Frankenberg, E., Lee, C., & Orfield, G. (January 2003). *A multiracial society with segregated schools: Are we losing the dream?* Cambridge, MA: The Civil Rights Project at Harvard University.

Frankenberg, E., Siegel-Hawley, G., & Wang, J. (2010). *Choice without equity: Charter school segregation and the need for civil rights standards.* Los Angeles, CA: The Civil Rights Projects/ Proyecto Derechos Civiles at UCLA; www.civilrightsproject.ucla.edu.

Fraser, N. (1997). *Justice interruptus: Critical reflections on the "postsocialist" condition.* New York: Routledge.

Freire, P. (2000). *Pedagogy of the oppressed* (30th anniversary ed.) (M.B. Ramos, Trans.). New York: Continuum. (Original work published 1968.)

Freire, P. (1973). *Education for critical consciousness.* New York: Seabury Press.

Frewing, D. (2001). The lives of migrant farmworkers. *Rethinking Schools*, 15(3). www. rethinkingschools.org/restrict.asp?path=archive/15_03/Farm153.shtml.

Fricker, M. (2007). *Epistemic injustice: Power and the ethics of knowing.* New York: Oxford University Press.

Garmon, M. (2004). Changing preservice teachers' attitudes/beliefs about diversity: What are the critical factors? *Journal of Teacher Education*, 55(3), 201–213.

Garvey, J. & Ignatiev, N. (1997). Toward a new abolitionism: A race traitor manifesto. In M. Hill (Ed.), *Whiteness: A critical reader* (pp. 346–349). New York: New York University Press.

Gaztambide-Fernández, R. (2009). *The best of the best: Becoming elite at an American boarding school.* Cambridge, MA: Harvard University Press.

Geertz, C. (1977). *The interpretation of cultures.* New York: Basic Books.

Gerring, J. (2007). *Case study research: Principles and practice.* New York: Cambridge University Press.

Gewirtz, S. (1998). Conceptualizing social justice in education: Mapping the territory. *Journal of Education Policy*, 13(4), 469–484.

Gillborn, D. (2008). *Racism and education.* London: Routledge.

Gillham, B. (2000). *Case study research methods.* New York: Continuum.

Giroux, H. (1992). Paulo Freire and the politics of postcolonialism. *Journal of Advanced Composition*, 12(1), 15–26.

Goodman, D. (2000a). Motivating people from privileged groups to support social justice. *Teachers College Record*, 102(6), 1061–1085.

Goodman, D. (2000b). *Promoting diversity and social justice: Educating people from privileged groups.* Thousand Oaks, CA: Sage Publications.

Gorski, P. (2006). Complicity with conservatism: The de-politicizing and re-politicizing of social justice education. *Intercultural Education*, 17(2), 162–177.

Grant, C. & Sleeter, C. (1986). Race, class, and gender in education research: An argument for integrative analysis. *Educational Researcher*, 56(2), 195–211.

Greene, M. (1995). *Releasing the imagination: Essays on education, the arts, and social change.* San Francisco: Jossey Bass.

Gutmann, A. & Thompson, D. (2004). *Why deliberative democracy?* Princeton, NJ: Princeton University Press.

Gutstein, E. (2003). Teaching and learning mathematics for social justice in an urban, Latino school. *Journal for Research in Mathematics Education*, 34(1), 37–73.

Gutstein, E. (2006). *Reading and writing the world with mathematics: Toward a pedagogy of social justice.* New York: Routledge.

Hackman, H.W. (2005). Five essential components for social justice education. *Equity & Excellence in Education*, 38(2), 103–109.

Halverson, R. (2004). Accessing, documenting, and communicating practical wisdom: The phronesis of school leadership practice. *American Journal of Education*, 111(1), 90–121.

Heinze, P. (2008). Let's talk about race, baby: How a white professor teaches white students about white privilege & racism. *Multicultural Education*, 16(1), 2–11.

Hernández-Sheets, R. (2000). Advancing the field or taking center stage: the White movement in multicultural education. *Educational Researcher*, 29(9), 29–35.

Hernández-Sheets, R. (2003). Competency vs. good intentions: Diversity ideologies and teacher potential. *Qualitative Studies in Education*, 16(1), 111–120.

Himley, M. (2004). Facing (up to) "the stranger" in community service learning. *College Composition and Communication*, 55(3), 416–438.

Hirsch, E.D. (1988). *Cultural literacy: What every American needs to know*. New York: Vintage Books.

hooks, b. (1994). *Teaching to transgress: Education as the practice of freedom*. London: Routledge.

Hout, M. (2008). How class works: Objective and subjective aspects of class since the 1970s. In A. Lareau & D. Conley (Eds.) *Social class: How does it work?* (pp. 25–64). New York: Russell Sage Foundation.

Howard, A. (2008). *Learning privilege: Lessons of power and identity in affluent schooling*. New York: Routledge.

Howard, A. & Gaztambide-Fernández, R. (Eds.) (2010). *Educating elites: Class privilege and educational advantage*. Lanham, MD: Rowman & Littlefield.

Howard, G. (1981). Multiethnic education in monocultural schools. In J. Banks & B. Shin (Eds.) *Multiethnic education* (pp. 117–127). Washington, DC: National Education Association.

Hurtado, A. (1996). *The color of privilege*. Ann Arbor, MI: University of Michigan Press.

Isaacs, J. (2007). *Economic mobility of black and white families*. Washington, DC: Economic Mobility Project, Pew Charitable Trust.

Johnson, A. (2006). *Privilege, power, and difference* (2nd ed.). New York: McGraw Hill.

Joyce, P. & Tutela, J. (2006). We make our road by talking: Preparing to do educational research. In J. Kincheloe & K. Tobin (Eds.) *Doing educational research: A handbook* (pp. 59–84). Rotterdam: Sense Publishers.

Karabel, J. (2006). *The chosen: The hidden history of admission and exclusion at Harvard, Yale, and Princeton*. New York: Mariner Books.

Kelly, G. (2006). Epistemology and educational research. In J.L. Green, G. Camilli, G., & P.B. Elmore (Eds.) *Complementary methods in educational research*, (pp. 33–56). Mahwah, NJ: Lawrence Erlbaum.

Khan, S.R. (2011). *Privilege: The making of an adolescent elite at St. Paul's School*. Princeton, NJ: Princeton University Press.

Kincheloe, J. (2005). *Critical constructivism*. New York: Peter Lang.

Kincheloe, J. & McLaren, P.L. (1994). Rethinking critical theory and qualitative research. In N.K. Denzin & Y.S. Lincoln (Eds.), *Handbook of qualitative research* (pp. 138–157). Thousand Oaks, CA: Sage Publications.

Kincheloe, J. & Steinberg, S. (1998). Addressing the crisis of whiteness: Reconfiguring white identity in a pedagogy of whiteness. In J. Kincheloe, S. Steinberg, N. Rodriguez, & R. Chennault (Eds.), *White reign* (pp. 3–29). New York: St. Martin's Griffin.

Kincheloe, J. & Tobin, K. (2006). *Doing educational research: A handbook*. Rotterdam: Sense Publishers.

Kingston, P.W. and Lewis, L.S. (Eds.) (1990). *The high-status track: Studies of elite schools and stratification*. Stanford, CA: Stanford University Press.

Kivel, P. (2002). How white people can serve as allies to people of color in the struggle to end racism. In P.S. Rothenberg's (Ed.), *White privilege: Essential readings on the other side of racism* (pp. 127–135). New York: Worth Publishers.

Kumashiro, K. (2002). *Troubling education*. New York: Routledge Falmer.

Kumashiro, K. (2004). *Against common sense: Teaching and learning towards social justice.* Routledge: New York.

Ladson-Billings, G. (1994). *The dreamkeepers: Successful teachers of African American children.* San Francisco: Jossey-Bass.

Ladson-Billings, G. (2006). From the achievement gap to the education debt: Understanding achievement in U.S. schools. *Educational Researcher, 35*(7), 3–12.

Lampert, K. (2005). *Traditions of compassion: From religious duty to social activism.* New York: Palgrave Macmillan.

Landsman, J. (2001). *A white teacher talks about race.* Lanham, MD: Rowman & Littlefield Education.

Lareau, A. (2003). *Unequal childhoods: Class, race, and family life.* Berkeley, CA: University of California Press.

Lareau, A. (2008). Taking stock of social class. In A. Lareau and D. Conley (Eds.) *Social class: How does it work?* (pp. 3–24). New York: Russell Sage Foundation.

Lave, J. (1988). *Cognition in practice: Mind, mathematics, and culture in everyday life.* New York: Cambridge University Press.

Lave, J. (1996). Teaching, as learning, in practice. *Mind, Culture, and Activity, 3*(3), 149–163.

Leistyna, P. (2009). Preparing for public life: Education, critical theory, and social justice. In W. Ayers, T. Quinn, & D. Stovall (Eds.) *Handbook on social justice in education* (pp. 51–58). New York: Routledge.

Leistyna, P. & Woodrum, A. (1996). Context and culture: What is critical pedagogy? In P. Leistyna, A. Woodrum, and S.A. Sherblom (Eds.), *Breaking free: The transformative power of critical pedagogy* (pp. 1–7). Cambridge, MA: Harvard Educational Review.

Leonardo, Z. (2009). *Race, whiteness, and education.* New York: Routledge.

Leont'ev, A. N. (1978). *Activity, consciousness and personality.* Englewood Cliffs, NJ: Prentice Hall.

Levine, M. (2008). *The price of privilege: How parental pressure and material advantage are creating a generation of disconnected and unhappy kids.* New York: HarperCollins.

Lincoln, Y.S. & Guba, E.G. (1985). *Naturalistic inquiry.* Thousand Oaks, CA: Sage Publications.

Lipman, P. (1998). *Race, class, and power in school restructuring.* Albany, NY: State University of New York Press.

Lipman, P. (2011). *The new political economy of urban education: Neoliberalism, race, and the right to the city.* New York: Routledge.

Lipsitz, G. (2002). The possessive investment in whiteness. In P.S. Rothenberg (Ed.) *White privilege: Essential readings on the other side of racism* (pp. 61–84). New York: Worth Publishers.

Luria, A.R. (1981). *Language and cognition.* New York: John Wiley & Sons.

Luthar, S.S. (2003). The culture of affluence: The psychological costs of material wealth. *Child Development, 74*(6), 1591–1593.

Manglitz, E. (2003). Challenging white privilege in adult education: A critical review of the literature. *Adult Education Quarterly, 53*, 119–134.

Marx, K. (1990). *Capital volume I* (2nd ed.) (B. Fowkes, Trans.). New York: Penguin Classics. (Original work published 1867.)

Mattick, P. (2011). *Business as usual: The economic crisis and the failure of capitalism.* London: Reaktion Books.

McArdle, N., Osypuk, T., & Acevedo-García, D. (2010). *Segregation and exposure to high-poverty schools in large metropolitan areas: 2008–2009*. Diversitydata.org Special Report. Retrieved from http://diversitydata.sph.harvard.edu/Publications/school_segregation_report.pdf.

McDonald, M. & Zeichner, K. (2009). Social justice teacher education. In W. Ayers, T. Quinn, & K. Stovall (Eds). *Handbook on social justice in education* (pp. 595–610). New York: Erlbaum Press.

McGee, C.A. & Banks, J.A. (1995). Equity pedagogy: An essential component of multicultural education. *Theory into Practice*, 34(3), 152–158.

McIntosh, P. (1990). White privilege: Unpacking the invisible knapsack. *Independent School*, 49, 31–36.

McIntosh, P. (1997). White privilege and male privilege: A personal account of coming to see correspondences through work in women's studies. In R. Delgado and Jean Stefancic (Eds.) *Critical white studies: Looking behind the mirror* (291–300). Philadelphia, PA: Temple University Press.

McLaren, P. (1998). *Life in schools: An introduction to critical pedagogy in the foundations of education*. Reading, MA: Addison Wesley Longman.

McLaren, P., Martin, G., Farahmandpur, R., & Jaramillo, N. (2004). Teaching in and against the empire: Critical pedagogy as revolutionary praxis. *Teacher Education Quarterly*, Winter, 131–153.

Meiers, D. & Wood, G. (2004). *Many children left behind: How the No Child Left Behind Act is damaging our children and our schools*. Boston: Beacon Press.

Meiners, E. (2007). *Right to be hostile: Schools, prisons, and the making of public enemies*. New York: Routledge.

Merriam, S.B. (1998). *Qualitative research and case study applications in education*. San Francisco: Jossey Bass.

Miel, A. & Kiester, E. (1967). *The shortchanged children of suburbia: What schools don't teach about human differences and what can be done about it*. New York: Institute of Human Relations Press, The American Jewish Committee.

Nespor, J. (2006). Finding patterns with field notes. In Green, J.L., Camilli, G., & Elmore, P.B. (Eds.) *Complementary methods in educational research*. Washington, DC: American Educational Research Association, 297–308.

Nieto, S. (2000). *Affirming diversity: The sociopolitical context of multicultural education*. New York: Longman.

Nin, A. (1971). *The Diary of Anaïs Nin* Vol. 4. Orlando, FL: Harcourt Brace Jovanovich.

Noddings, N. (1984). *Caring: A feminine approach to ethics and moral education*. Berkeley, CA: University of California Press.

North, C. (2006). More than words? Delving into the substantive meaning(s) of "social justice" in education. *Review of Educational Research*, 76(4), 507–535.

North, C. (2008). What is all this talk about "social justice"? Mapping the terrain of education's latest catchphrase. *The Teachers College Record*, 110(6), 1182–1206.

North, C. (2009). *Teaching for social justice? Voices from the front lines*. Boulder, CO: Paradigm Publishers.

Nussbaum, M. (1992). Human functioning and social justice: In defense of Aristotelian essentialism. *Political Theory*, 20(2), 202–246.

Oakes, J. (2005). *Keeping track: How schools structure inequality* (2nd ed.). New Haven, CT: Yale University Press.

O'Connell, M. (2009). *Compassion: Loving our neighbor in an age of globalization.* Maryknoll, NY: Orbis Books.

Orfield, G. (2009). *Reviving the goal of an integrated society: A 21st century challenge.* Los Angeles: The Civil Rights Project/Proyecto Derechos Civiles at UCLA.

Orfield, G., Frankenberg, E., & Garces, L.M. (2008). Statement of social scientists of research on school desegregation to the U.S. Supreme Court in *Parents v. Seattle School District and Meredith v. Jefferson County. Urban Review,* 40(1), 96–136.

Orozco, R. (2012). Racism and power: Arizona politicians' use of the discourse of anti-Americanism against Mexican American Studies. *Hispanic Journal of Behavioral Sciences,* 34(1), 43-60.

Parker, W. (2003). *Teaching democracy: Unity and diversity in public life.* New York: Teachers College Press.

Pattillo, M. (2008). Race, class, and neighborhoods. In A. Lareau & D. Conley (Eds.) *Social class: How does it work?* (pp. 264–292). New York: Russell Sage Foundation.

Payne, R. (1996). *A framework for understanding poverty.* Highlands, TX: aha! Press.

Penuel, W.R. & Wertsch, J.V. (1995). Vygotsky and identity formation: Sociocultural approach. *Educational Psychology,* 30, 83–92.

Peoples-Wessinger, N. (1994). Celebrating our differences—fostering ethnicity in homogeneous settings. *Journal of Physical Education, Recreation, and Dance,* 65(9), 62–68.

Pickett, K. & Wilkinson, R. (2009). *The spirit level: Why greater equality makes societies stronger.* London: Bloomsbury Press.

Pikkety, T. & Saez, E. (2003). Income inequality in the United States: 1913–1998. *Quarterly Journal of Economics,* 118, 1–39.

Pollock, M. (2004). *Colormute: Race talk dilemmas in an American school.* Princeton, NJ: Princeton University Press.

Pollock, M. (Ed.) (2008). *Everyday anti-racism: Getting real about race in schools.* New York: New Press.

Republican Party of Texas (2012). *Report of platform committee.* Retrieved from www.texas-gop.org/about-the-party.

Rodriguez, N. (2000). Projects of whiteness in a critical pedagogy. In Rodriguez, N. & Villaverde, L.E. (Eds.) *Dismantling privilege: Pedagogy, politics, and whiteness* (pp. 1–24). New York: Peter Lang Publishing.

Rogoff, B. (2003). *The cultural nature of human development.* Oxford: Oxford University Press.

Rogoff, B. & Lave, J. (Eds.) (1984). *Everyday cognition: Its development in social context.* Cambrdige, MA: Harvard University Press.

Roth, W.M. & Lee, Y.J. (2007). 'Vygotsky's neglected legacy': Cultural-Historical Activity Theory. *Review of Educational Research,* 77(2), 186–232.

Rothenberg, P.S. (Ed.) (2002). *White privilege: Essential readings on the other side of racism.* New York: Worth Publishers.

Rothstein, R. (2012). A comment on Bank of America/Countrywide's discriminatory mortgage lending and its implications for racial segregation. Economic Policy Institute Briefing Paper 335. Washington, DC: Economic Policy Institute.

Sawhill, I. & Morton, J. (2007). *Economic mobility: Is the American dream alive and well?* Washington, DC: Economic Mobility Project, Pew Charitable Trust.

Sayer, A. (2005). *The moral significance of class.* Cambridge, UK: Cambridge University Press.

Schapiro, S. (1999). Toward a pedagogy of the "oppressor": A Freirian approach to anti-sexist education with men. In S. Schapiro (Ed.) *Higher education for democracy.* New York: Peter Lang.

Schrag, F. (1995). *Back to basics: Fundamental educational questions reexamined.* New York: Jossey-Bass.

Schultz, B. (2008). *Spectacular things happen along the way: Lessons from an urban classroom.* New York: Teachers College Press.

Schwartz, B. (2000). Self-determination: The tyranny of freedom. *American Psychologist,* 55, 79–88.

Scribner, S. (1990). A sociocultural approach to the study of the mind. In G. Greenberg & E. Tobach (Eds.) *Theories of the evolution of knowing* (pp. 107–120). Hillsdale, NJ: Lawrence Erlbaum.

Seider, S. (2008). Bad things could happen: How fear impedes social responsibility in privileged adolescents. *Journal of Adolescent Research,* 23(6), 647–666.

Seider, S. (2009). Resisting obligation: How privileged adolescents conceive of their obligation to others. Paper presentation at AERA, San Diego, CA, April 15.

Sharkey, P. (2009). *Neighborhoods and the black–white mobility gap.* Washington, DC: Economic Mobility Project, Pew Charitable Trust.

Shor, I. (1992). *Empowering education: Critical teaching for social change.* Chicago: University of Chicago Press.

Sleeter, C.E. & Grant, C.A. (2007). *Making choices for multicultural education: Five approaches to race, class and gender.* New York: Wiley, John, & Sons.

Stake, R. (1995). *The art of case study research.* Thousand Oaks, CA: Sage Publications.

Staples, M. (2005). Integrals and equity. *Rethinking Schools,* 19(3), 50–52.

Stevens, M. (2007). *Creating a class: College admissions and the education of elites.* Cambridge, MA: Harvard University Press.

Swaminathan, R. (2007). Educating for the 'real world': The hidden curriculum of community service-learning. *Equity & Excellence in Education,* 40(2), 134–143.

Swift, A. (2003). *How not to be a hypocrite: School choice for the morally perplexed parent.* New York: Routledge.

Templeton, A.R. (1999). Human races: A genetic and evolutionary perspective. *American Anthropologist,* 100(3), 632–650.

Thompson, B. (2002). Multiracial feminism: Recasting the chronology of Second Wave feminism. *Feminist Studies,* 28(2), 336–360.

Tobin, K. (2006). Qualitative research in classrooms: Pushing the boundaries of theory and methodology. In J. Kincheloe and K. Tobin (Eds.) *Doing educational research: A handbook* (pp. 15–58). Rotterdam: Sense Publishers.

Valenzuela, A. (1999). *Subtractive schooling: U.S. Mexican youth and the politics of caring.* Albany, NY: State University of New York Press.

van Gorder, A.C. (2007). Pedagogy for the children of the oppressors. *Journal of Transformative Education,* 5(1), 8–32.

Vygotsky, L.S. (1978). *Mind in society: The development of higher psychological processes.* Boston: Harvard University Press.

Wade, R. (2001). Social action in the social studies: From the ideal to the real. *Theory into Practice,* 40(1), 23–28.

Weis, L., Fine, M., & Dimitriadis, G. (2009). Towards a critical theory of method in shifting times. In M. Apple, W. Au, & L.A. Gandin (Eds.) *The Routledge international handbook of critical education* (pp. 437–448). New York: Routledge.

Wertsch, J.V. (1998). *Mind as action.* New York: Oxford University Press.

Westheimer, J. & Kahne, J. (1998). Education for action: Preparing youth for participatory democracy. In W. Ayers, J.A. Hunt, & T. Quinn (Eds.), *Teaching for social justice* (pp. 1–19). New York: New Press.

Westheimer, J. & Kahne, J. (2002). Educating the "good" citizen: The politics of school-based democracy education programs. Paper presented at the annual meeting of the American Political Science Association, Boston, MA, August.

Westheimer, J. & Kahne, J. (2004). What kind of citizen? The politics of educating for democracy. *American Educational Research Journal*, 41(2), 237–269.

Whitty, G. (1985). *Sociology and school knowledge*. London: Routledge.

Willis, P. (1981). *Learning to labor: How working class kids get working class jobs*. New York: Columbia University Press.

Wilson-Doenges, G. (2000). An exploration of sense of community and fear of crime in gated communities. *Environment & Behavior*, 32, 597–611.

Wise, T. (2002). Thoughts on acknowledging and challenging whiteness. In P.S. Rothenberg's (Ed.) *White privilege: Essential readings on the other side of racism* (pp. 107–110). New York: Worth Publishers.

Wise, T. (2008). *White like me: Reflections on a race from a privileged son*. Berkeley, CA: Soft Skull Press.

Wright, E.O. (1997). *Class counts: Comparative studies in class analysis*. Cambridge, UK: Cambridge University Press.

Wright, E.O. (2008). Logics of class analysis. In A. Lareau & D. Conley (Eds.) *Social class: How does it work?* (pp. 329–349). New York: The Russell Sage Foundation.

Wright, E.O. (2010). *American society: How it really works*. New York: Norton.

Wright, E.O. & Rogers, J. (2010). *American society: How it really works*. New York: Norton.

Yin, R.K. (2003). *Case study research: Design and methods*. Thousand Oaks, CA: Sage Publications.

Yin, R. (2006). Case study methods. In J. Green, G. Camilli, & P.B. Elmore (Eds.). *Handbook of complementary methods in education research*. Mahwah, NJ: Lawrence Erlbaum, 111–122.

Youdell, D. (2006). *Impossible bodies, impossible selves*. Dordrecht, Netherlands: Springer.

Young, I.M. (1990). *Justice and the politics of difference*. Princeton, NJ: Princeton University Press.

Young, I.M. (2006). Responsibility and global justice: A social connection model. *Social Philosophy and Policy*, 23(1), 102–130.

Young, M.F.D. (2008). From constructivism to realism in the sociology of the curriculum. *Review of Research in Education*, 32, 1–28.

Zeichner, K. & Flessner, R. (2009). Educating teachers for critical education. In M. Apple, W. Au, & L. Armando Gandin (Eds). *International handbook of critical education*. New York: Routledge. New York: Erlbaum/Routledge.

INDEX